MY HEA
LOVE
IN MY
LANGUAGE

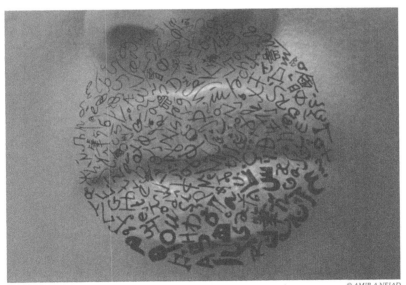

MY HEART LOVES IN MY LANGUAGE

POEMS & STORIES FROM SWANSEA

Editors
TOM CHEESMAN
JENI WILLIAMS
FILIZ ÇELIK

Hafan Books

Hafan Books

c/o Tom Cheesman
Swansea University
Wales   SA2 8PP   UK

lulu.com/hafan   t.cheesman@swansea.ac.uk

All proceeds go to
Swansea Bay Asylum Seekers Support Group

My Heart Loves in My Language is number 7
in the 'Refugees Writing in Wales' series

© the contributors 2016

Printed by Lulu.com in 2017

ISBN 9780995496644

Cover image: handwriting by Xuecheng Cai.
Frontispiece design © Amir A Nejad, including the logo
        of Pen International.
Calligraphy on p. 66 from calltowardslight.blogspot.co.uk

Hafan Books gratefully acknowledges support from the
'Cross-Language Dynamics: Reshaping Community' project
at Swansea University, funded by the Arts and Humanities
Research Council under the Open World Research Initiative.

Contents

Part 1: Cross-Language Dynamics: Stories of (Mis)Interpreting and Translating

Interpreters in the Community: More than Language

Acknowledgments

Most of the stories in Part 1 of this book were told by people in Swansea to Professor Tom Cheesman and Dr Filiz Çelik, in 2017, during their work on a research project on 'Cross-Language Dynamics', based in the Department of Modern Languages, Translation and Interpreting, at Swansea University.

Most of the poems in Part 2 were created in workshops led by Dr Jeni Williams (Senior Lecturer in Literature and Creative Writing at University of Wales Trinity Saint David, Lampeter), supported in 2017 by the research project. The poems by Daad Lubeck and Xuecheng Cai emerged from the 'Mother Tongue, Other Tongue' writing workshop series at the Glynn Vivian Art Gallery, led by artist in residence Professor Sharon Morris (Slade School of Fine Art, London).

Our project was funded by the Arts and Humanities Research Council, as part of the Open World Research Initiative, within the consortium project titled 'Cross-Language Dynamics: Reshaping Community', based at Manchester University.

Our project has involved (among other things) investigating interpreting services and 'interpreting in the community' within community organisations. We also convened discussion forums with interpreters. Extracts from notes on conversations, interviews and discussions appear in this book. As well as supporting Jeni's poetry workshops, we also staged a series of 10 public events during April, May and June 2017, with multilingual writers and performers from Swansea, the rest of Wales, the UK and abroad. These 'Volcano Fridays', held at Volcano Theatre, were organised in collaboration with the writers' organisation Wales PEN Cymru (part of PEN International), Tŷ Tawe Sesiwn Werin (the Ty Tawe folk club), and Swansea Women's Asylum and Refugee Group. Special thanks to Huw Dylan Owen and others, for the music, and to Lubna and Saba, for the food.

Organisations which collaborated and contributed to the project include: African Community Centre, Ethnic Youth Support Team, Swansea Bay Asylum Seekers Support Group, Swansea City of Sanctuary, Unity in Diversity, as well as the National Waterfront Museum, the Glynn Vivian Art Gallery and last not least Volcano Theatre.

To everyone in these organisations who helped: thank you all!

Above all we thank all the contributors, named and unnamed, for sharing their stories and poems.

Fond greetings to Sylvie Hoffmann: some of her 'found poems' about interpreting are included here, having appeared in previous Hafan Books anthologies.

We plan to publish an extended edition of this book in 2019. Please get in touch if you would like to contribute a story or poem. It doesn't matter what languages you speak or read or write or don't.

Introduction

Tom Cheesman and Filiz Çelik

After the horrific Grenfell Tower fire on 14 June 2017, it was 8 days before Kensington Council put up any notices providing advice to survivors: and those notices were in English only. A lot of the survivors are not fluent in English. It was 22 days before any notices appeared in Arabic, Kensington's second language. Volunteers tried to plug the communications gap. More than 20 languages are spoken by the survivors. But organising translators and interpreters should not be too difficult or costly for a public authority. "The council and the government have no excuse. It's almost as if they don't understand their capital city's history," wrote Lily Allen and Sam Duckworth,[1] demanding: "Help the survivors by giving them the choice. Allow families to understand together. Everything has been difficult to comprehend – please don't make the information you provide impossible to understand."

Multilingualism is a challenge for public authorities, not just in emergencies, and not just in London. Swansea and Wales are now massively multilingual too. All of us – citizens and newcomers alike – are living in language diversity. We need to adapt.

Swansea has become a cosmopolitan city in the past fifteen years or so. More than 150 languages are spoken among schoolchildren in the city. People you meet on

---

[1] 'Speak to Grenfell survivors in language they can understand', *The Guardian*, 16 July 2017.

the street or in shops, at the GP clinic or the Job Centre can be from literally anywhere in the world, speaking any of the world's languages.

People come to live in Swansea, short-term or long-term, for work, for love, for study, by chance. Or for survival. One big factor making Swansea more diverse, since the year 2000, is the 'dispersal' of asylum-seekers from South East England, by the Home Office.

There are nearly 3,000 accommodation places for asylum-seekers in Wales, nearly 900 in Swansea. You claim asylum and you are sent here to wait for the Home Office to decide your case: maybe just a few weeks or months, or you may wait for years and years. You could come from anywhere in Asia and Africa, the Middle East and the former Soviet Union – even from South America. You have escaped from war, civil war, persecution because of your ethnic identity, or your sexuality, or your political or religious beliefs; and (or) because you were displaced from your home by ecological and economic disaster, social violence, organised crime, gender violence. About two thirds of asylum-seekers in the UK are eventually 'accepted' by the Home Office: granted protection, given sanctuary.

The longer you stay in Swansea, the more likely you are to settle here. So the city's ethnic, religious, linguistic and cultural diversity steadily grows. More and more refugees are UK citizens and think of themselves as Swansea Jacks and Jills.

Most speak several languages: multilingualism is normal in most of the world. Many recognise Welsh language politics as a familiar situation: colonised minorities resisting linguistic oppression. Stories in this book by Kurdish and Amazigh speakers illustrate that. Many, when they get here, speak less than perfect English; some none at all. Even if they do speak English fluently, their accent, their 'variety' of the global language can be hard to understand for the natives here, and that works both ways. Reading and writing is another set of issues. So language is often a barrier. People on both sides of the barrier will ideally learn each other's languages.

Otherwise, we need translation and interpreting to be able to communicate. ('Translation' refers to written language; 'interpreting' refers to speech.)[2] Employing a professional – like a court interpreter – or using a phone service (like LanguageLine, used by the NHS) – is often not an option. Someone has to pay. As Grenfell Tower illustrates, the need must be recognised and budgets must be allocated.

Interpreting with no money means improvised problem-solving, with help from family, friends, passers-by, mobile apps, and hopefully a good sense of humour. This can be better than using a professional interpreter, because volunteers tend to know the people concerned, understand the context, and can act as advocates, advisors and moral supporters – not just translate the words.

During 2017, we researched 'interpreting in the

---

[2] At a refugee drop-in, Tom was asked: "I hear you have a new project all about entrepreneurs...?" It took a while to work it out: it was a misunderstanding of 'interpreters'...

community' in Swansea. We talked with people who act (unpaid and untrained) as interpreters, and people who need interpreters, mainly in places where people seeking sanctuary gather at drop-ins and other services provided by African Community Centre, Ethnic Youth Support Team, Swansea Bay Asylum Seekers Support Group, and Unity in Diversity. We asked people to tell us stories about their experiences with language barriers, language learning, and language problem-solving. **Part 1** of this book reproduces some of the stories we heard.

These stories tell of the challenges people face and – mostly – resilience in coping. They make clear that the language services on offer are far from adequate. There are not enough opportunities to learn English (some learners give up in despair), interpreters are often unavailable when needed, and the downsides of relying on volunteers are made clear too.

A Welsh Assembly Member reports families coming to see her for advice, relying on children as young as 5 to interpret. Organisations like the Job Centre rely on untrained volunteers; clients report being told to bring their own interpreter, i.e. a friend who speaks better English. In the NHS, some doctors don't like using LanguageLine, for various reasons. Some doctors tell patients to learn better English. Some patients may agree that in the long run, that is their best option, but meanwhile language barriers are preventing people from getting adequate care, if they don't understand the language and how the NHS system works.

Interpreters and bilingual classroom support

workers give glimpses into their work, which goes far beyond simple translating. Some of them are fully trained professionals and work for pay; not all. All give extra time voluntarily, acting as human bridges between their mother-tongue language communities and the wider society. They build cross-language, multilingual community, one conversation at a time.

Conversations across languages need to be creative and personal. **Part 2** presents poems, some of which are directly 'about' language – including Hannah Sabatia's poem 'The Sound of My Language', which gave us the book's title. All of these poems are 'cross-language' creations. They came out of creative writing workshops with about a dozen refugee women who at least speak twenty different languages between them. Jeni Williams and Sharon Morris helped the participants to create works of art in the English language: poems in which the writer connects with readers – that is, you – as a flesh and blood person, not a 'case' or a statistic.

As Jeni says in her introduction to Part 2, the kind of English that refugees get to know is the English of law and administration: a cold, heartless language of 'fact' and 'proof', demanding that they 'authenticate' a story that fits Home Office categories. It's a language in which they cannot be themselves – they cannot even be a real person. Their own languages, their mother tongues, the languages their hearts speak in and love in, carry emotional force, personal memories. In the poetry workshops, English begins to become a new heart language.

This book can be read as a journey from being stuck

behind the language barrier, feeling you have 'a glass put on you', being unable to speak and connect with people – through experiences of translating and interpreting – to using English as a language of free, creative, connecting expression. A journey from being a stranger here, to being a citizen of a cosmopolitan, multilingual Swansea, Wales, UK: a member of a community open to the world and to each other.

T.C., J.W., F.Ç – Swansea, September 2017

Sözcüklerden yoruldum   I'm Tired of All the Words

Meltem Arıkan is a feminist activist and an award-winning novelist and dramatist from Istanbul. She has been living in exile since 2014, in Wales. Her interactive political drama 'Mi Minor', staged in Istanbul in 2012-13, led to a state-sponsored hate campaign which was so threatening that she was forced to leave Turkey together with her collaborators, the celebrated actress Pınar Öğün and director Memet Ali Alabora. Now they work together in Cardiff, as BeAware Productions. Meltem's text was translated by Pınar Öğün and Filiz Çelik.

Sözcükler, kelimeler, anlamlar, kimlik, benlik, ben olmak, ben olamamak, ait olmak, ait olamamak, ifade etmek, sessiz kalmak, konuşmak, yazmak, dil, dili kullanmak, dili kullanamamak, kabullenmek, sessiz kalmak, sıkışmak, sıkışmak, sıkışmak....

Words, sentences, meanings, identity, being, being me, not being me, to belong, not to belong, to express, to be quiet, to speak, to write, language, to utter language, not to utter language, to accept, to remain silent, to be crushed, to be crushed, to be crushed…

Kendimi anlamak için sürekli yazdım. Geçmişimi, ailemi, anılarımı, hayallerimi, hayal kırıklıklarımı. Kimi zaman ilmek ilmek söktüm kendimi, kimi zaman kırılan parçalara böldüm, neden, niçin, nasıl, nerede, sorularının yanıtlarını bulana kadar kendimi yaprak yaprak soydum.

In order to understand myself I've always written.

My past, my family, my memories, my dreams, my disappointments. Sometimes knot after knot I untied myself, sometimes I broke myself into pieces, leaf after leaf I undressed myself until I found out the answers to the questions why, what for, how and where.

Kat kat giyinmek ihtiyacında olan toplum için de sakıncalı ve tehlikeli oldum. Soyundukça şeffaflaştım, şeffaflaştıkça kırılganlaştım, kırılganlaştıkça güçlendim. Düşüncelerimi her zaman tüm açıklığıyla dile getirdim, hiç bir zaman kabul edilmek adına inanmadığım şeyleri söylemedim.

At the end, I became inconvenient and dangerous for the society that needs to be wrapped in layers of clothing. The more I undress the more I become transparent, the more I become transparent the more I become fragile, the more I become fragile the more I grow strong. I've always expressed my thoughts crystal clear; I've never said anything I don't believe in, just to be accepted.

Ancak duygularımı tüm açıklığıyla ifade etmek konusunda tam bir İngiliz olduğumu itiraf etmeliyim. O nedenle de edebiyatın sunduğu o sınırsız dünyada çok mutlu oldum... Edebiyat aracılığı bireylere kat kat giysileriyle aslında kendilerine ne kadar yabancı olduklarını algılatmaya çalışırken kendi duygularımı da karakterler aracılığı ile ifade etmenin rahatlığında yazdım. Anladım, yazdım, anladım, yazdım...

But I must admit I'm so English when it's about letting my emotions show. For that reason, I found happiness in the limitless world of literature... In literature, trying to show people how they become alienated from themselves under those layers of clothing, it comforted me to write about my own emotions by disguising them all behind the characters of my novels. I understood, I wrote, I understood, I wrote...

'Anlamak' benim için hep sözcüklerle kurduğum ilişkiyle bağlantılı oldu. Benim için sözcükler hep çok önemli oldu. Sözcükler, dil, dili kullanma biçimi, dilin duyguları anlatabilme verimliliği...

For me, 'to understand' has always been related to my relationship with words. For me words have always been vital. Words, language, the ways of using the language, the productivity of the language for expressing emotions...

Tarihin ilk başlarında, bugün anlaşmamızı sağlayan dillerin temelini oluşturan ilk heceleri kadınlar çıkarmıştır. Bu heceler sürekli evde, hayvanlarlarla ilgilenen kadınların hayvan seslerini taklitlerinden yola çıkarak çıkardığı seslerle oluşmuş. Ma, Me, Mo gibi...

In the beginning of human history it was women who expressed and built the foundation of the first syllables of all languages which we use today to communicate. Women, who spent time at home, on the land and with animals, began to imitate the voices of animals and that was how these syllables came to life. Ma, Me, Mo for example...

Kadınlar bu sesler aracılığıyla önce bebekleri sonra da birbirleriyle iletişim kurmuşlar. Av peşinde koşan adamlar ise bu heceleri daha sonra kadınlardan ve çocuklardan öğrenmişlerdir. Yazısız tarih kadınların sesleriyle başlamış olsa da, bu heceler daha sonra sözcüklere, sözcükler tümcelere, tümceler kavramlara, kavramlarsa dillere dönüşmüş. Kadınların anlaşmak için buldukları basit yöntemi geliştiren erkeklerle oluşan diller artık bizlerin ayrılmaz birer parçası olmuştur.

Through these sounds women first communicated with their babies and then with each other. Men, who were chasing after prey, learnt these syllables later than women. Unwritten history had begun with the sounds of women, but in time syllables turned into words, words into sentences, sentences into concepts, concepts into language. Men, who developed the simple communication method found by women, created the basis of conflict and complexity using these sounds.

Diller geliştikçe kimliğimizin şekillenmesinden, duygularımız ifade etme biçimimizden, aidiyet duygumuza kadar bizi varoluşumuzu belirleyen temel etmenlerden biri olmuştur.

As languages developed, they have become a fundamental component of what determines our existence, from how we express our feelings to our sense of belonging.

Bir yandan kendinizi ve etrafımızı anlamamıza yarayan dil, diğer yandan da bizi hem kendimizden hem de başkalarından ayırmaya, kimi zaman sınırlamaya başlamıştır. Anlaşmak için kullanılan dil anlaşamamanın da nedeni olmaya başlamıştır.

The language that helps us understand ourselves and our environment began to separate us from ourselves and our environment and at times restrict us. The language used to understand each other began to be the cause of not understanding each other.

Diller geliştikçe, dillerle yaratılan konseptler, kavramlar geliştikçe ne yazık ki insanlar birbirlerini daha iyi anlamamakta tam tersi sözcükler, kavramlara, kavramlar inançlara ve ideolojilere dönüştükçe artık insan duygularıyla olan bağlarını bile yitirmeye başladı diye düşünüyorum.

As languages and the concepts that emerged from languages have developed, they no longer help people to understand each other better but on the contrary, as words turned into concepts and concepts into beliefs and beliefs into ideologies they have lost their essential connection to human emotions.

O nedenle kimi zaman keşke hepimiz dillerimizden ve sözcüklerimizden biraz yorulsak ve onların ötesinde birbirimizi anlamamın bir yolunu bulsak diyorum...

For that reason, sometimes I wish we would all get a little tired of our language and words and find a way to understand each other beyond them…

PART 1

CROSS-LANGUAGE DYNAMICS

STORIES OF
(MIS)INTERPRETING
AND TRANSLATING

Almost Lost in Translation

Murat Kaya (Mediterranean Restaurant, Mumbles) told this story to F.Ç.

First year of my marriage – I'm Turkish and my wife's a Swansea Jill – I didn't understand most of what I was told. Swansea was a city of sounds that didn't make sense. All I understood was when people said "Galatasaray" *(the football team from Istanbul)*. Everyone I met said "Galatasaray" back then, because they won the UEFA Cup in 2000.

One day I was home alone and a Turkish friend of mine came round. He said, you must be bored, let's go out, and then you can meet your wife later when she finishes work.

So I called my wife. What I said was, my friend's here and he thinks I'm bored and he's taking me out. That's what I meant to say. My wife hung up on me.

I thought we'd been disconnected, so I tried again. I said the same thing and she hung up again.

I didn't go out. I couldn't understand why my wife was upset.

She eventually came home, distraught: what she thought I had said was, I was bored with her, so I was going off with my friend.

I almost lost my wife in translation.

A Glass Put on You

Interview at the community drop-in of Swansea Bay Asylum Seekers Support Group, by T.C.

– Can you tell me something about your feelings about language…
– Yes, I want to tell you about language. I've been in the UK nearly 5 years and I had no opportunity to learn English.
– But your English is good, you have a good accent…
– But I can only speak like this: very simple, everyday conversation. I cannot understand difficult things, important things. I cannot have a conversation with you about politics, philosophy, science, important things. All the time I'm just learning on YouTube, I try to find lessons and practise, practise, practise. I have never been to any English class. I am not confident about my language. If someone asks, "How long have you been here", and I say, "5 years", then it's a big question mark, why I can't speak?

Now, after 5 years waiting, at last I have a visa. But I'm worried about my age, I'm 35, I lost 5 years. I couldn't do anything! Job, work, study, nothing! I've been here in Swansea a few months. Now I'm in the queue for a College course in English. In London, I couldn't do any course. Because my case was refused. I lived with my auntie for 3 and a half years. I was homeless on the street for 6 months. It's a good … good for the Home Office, but not for me.

All door was closed on me. No language, it's like a

glass put on you. A big glass, coming over, down on you… I can't communicate, I see people, I can't touch them, they can't touch me. I'm inside the glass. You understand?

I'm getting… talking about these years… I punched the wall! Yes, I punched the wall. Punched, with this hand! I had two operations on my hand. My hand is disabled. It's hard to explain. I was under the pressure. I like study, education, communicate with educated people. I couldn't do anything.

If They Send Me Back

Interview by F.Ç.

A lot of things happened to me, I don't like talking about them because no one believes me... and sometime, I think maybe if I speak good English they understand me, I don't know... I have counselling here, I had interpreter, she was nice, you know from my country, she was not like the interpreters on the phone... As an asylum seeker, you don't know what is going to happen tomorrow... I am thinking about the past, I don't want to but I think about it... I feel afraid when someone is walking behind me, I feel afraid that something is happening to my mother... I want to learn more English but my mind is not accepting new learning, because I don't know if Home Office will accept my case. If they send me back, what good is to speak English...

At the College

Recorded by Sylvie Hoffmann

– How is your English coming along?
– I must!

Chinese Seniors

Community interpreter Yen Yen Lai speaks Malay, Mandarin and Cantonese (from her home country) and taught herself Hakka, by speaking to Chinese migrants here in Wales. On top of paid work, she often acts as a volunteer interpreter for the Chinese In Wales Association (formerly Swansea Chinese Community Co-op Centre).

Many Chinese people have lived here for decades, but they speak no English at all. As minority migrants here, they felt that they better work hard in silence instead of mingling with people. They spent their whole lives working, in the kitchens of Chinese takeaways, or at home with the family, only speaking Chinese, but now they have retired. When necessary I accompany them to the doctor or the hospital, to support and interpret, as a volunteer. The GPs and consultants look at their file to see how long the Chinese people have been living in the UK, and they ask: "Why can't you speak English?" It's very insulting to the elderly patients. They are senior citizens who have worked hard all their lives, for as much as 40 years, but they lacked opportunities to learn English due to their heavy work schedules, isolation, and the close-knit nature of the community and culture.

Fast and Strong

Interview by F.Ç.

I speak Tigrinya, the national language of Eritrea. During 12 years of education you study some English. I can write and read English. The problem is I can't speak well, I can't listen well. I know vocabulary. Only my problem is to speak and listen. Especially for white people I cannot speak and listen well. I know my problem. My problem is PRON... PRO... NAN... TICATION.... NOOO... Wait... PROO-UNCI-ATIOOON... PRO... NON... CISION...

White people speak fast and strong. In my country I studied a lot of subjects, History, Geography, Mathematics... But here people don't understand my English.

I said to one of the English teachers that white people are MODEEIN. She didn't understand me. I explained to her: like, new... you know, like, better. She taught me that it was with an R, like MODERRN. For me the R is silent. I can speak but people don't understand me.

My Memory is Finished

Interview by F.Ç.

I come from Iran. I arrived here in 2013. I started going to English classes. I wanted to learn English. I wanted to learn English because I like to speak to people, make friends, and find a good job. But sometimes I think my memory is finished, because I am not young any more, I am 42. When I can't speak with somebody I'll be very sad. I decided to cut my study English and I've stopped to go study at College and I've stopped learning.

Repeat Please!

Interview by F.Ç.

I'm from Albania, I'm a Christian Albanian, I speak Albanian and a little bit of English. I've a brother in London but the Home Office won't let me stay close to him, they sent me here, Swansea. I miss London. London has a huge Albanian population. I feel very lonely here; there's no one from my culture, from my country.

I live in a house with three other guys; two from Iran and one from Eritrea. One of the guys from Iran is a Christian, the other two guys are Muslim. All their English is beginners level, it's difficult to communicate. I want to talk to them. They never understand what I'm saying, everything I say, every question I ask they respond: REPEAT PLEASE! I try to say it in different words so they can understand, but my English isn't that good. I try to get the right words but it doesn't happen.

Sorani/Farsi, Welsh/English, Sunni/Shi'a

Interview by T.C.

My mother language is Kurdish: Sorani. That's what we spoke at home in the village. Me and my brother didn't speak any Persian [*the official language of Iran, also called Farsi*] until we went to school. We started talking to each other in Persian. Talking Farsi was fun, exciting, it felt like something different, something new, we were another person.

But what they teach at school and talking to people, it's different, same as with English.

They don't force everyone to speak Farsi. But you have to learn it. It's like for Welsh people: to understand everyone, they must speak English.

Religion makes people more different than language. The Persian (Shi'a) teacher told us everyone must follow their religion. I was surprised. They told us to study religion, they brought us books to read which said things like: Sunnis pray like the ... what's that big black and white bird? ... the stork on top of the tree.* Or: Never eat food with Sunnis or Christians off the same tablecloth – it's haram (sinful). I was surprised they said those things. The teacher said: This is the true book... Shi'a and Sunni, they both make religion into politics. I don't pray now. I read a lot...

During prayer (standing up), Shi'a Muslims usually place their hands at the sides of their body; Sunni Muslims cross their hands over their chest.

Progress

The interviewee is from Iraq, about 30 years old, and was studying in the UK when his family became refugees, fleeing to Turkey, so he had no home to go back to. He was living in a hostel in Swansea when F.Ç. interviewed him – he had recently been granted refugee status and immediately became homeless, as often happens.

I wake up and wash and then go to the breakfast room and there I eat bread, butter (past its sell-by date), and jam. I ask them: "Can you please make a boiled egg for breakfast?" They say: "No, sorry, we cannot afford it." I give them everything the Job Centre gives me.

I can speak English now. So I can ask them if I can please have a boiled egg. I couldn't speak English when I arrived in this country. I was at the border control at Heathrow Airport and I thought I could speak English, but I couldn't. In Iraq they teach us how to read and write English, but not how to speak. So I couldn't ask them then if I can please have asylum in the UK.

Waistcoats

Interview by T.C.

I'm a volunteer in a charity shop. Sometimes people ask me for something but I can't understand them, they talk very fast, I find myself trapped because I don't understand their word. Sometimes English in Wales sounds like German: "CH-how are CH-you?" *[imitating a very harsh, throaty, guttural accent]*. I say: I'm not an English person, please explain with different words, and afterwards they give me a clue, and I understand. I carry on and keep learning.

One time a lady came in the shop and said: "I want a waistcoat!" And I said: "What's that?" I know 'waist' and I know 'coat' but I'd never heard 'waistcoat' before, I couldn't imagine what it was. I asked her: "Is it a coat like yours?" She said: "Why are you working in this shop if you don't know that?" She was quite aggressive. Some people are not patient, it's like they're electricity, don't want to wait. Why are people like that? They come in the shop, pick some clothes, down like that *[mimes throwing clothes onto the shop counter]* ...

The day after this conversation, I asked an Iranian man if he had a story to tell about language. He looked blank, and I told him the waistcoat story. He said: "Oh, just yesterday, you see I'm going to a wedding tomorrow, I had my suit and I was in a shop looking for a waistcoat to match my suit, but I didn't know that word, I had to mime it on my body, and the assistant was laughing, but he was very nice..."

Nylon Bag

Interview by F.Ç.

I came to UK 10 years ago. I was trafficked here. I fell in love with a man, he said life would be better in the UK and if I went with him, he'd make sure my mom would be taken care of in Nigeria too. He made me work very hard, I worked two jobs all the time and I was forced into doing things I didn't like. I don't like to talk about that now. My children were born here, I was looking after them and working, I gave all I earned to him, I had to.

English is a national language in Nigeria, it's one of our mother tongues. Still, it was sometimes difficult to communicate when I arrived in this country. For example, once I was shopping at this grocery store and I asked the cashier for a nylon bag. She asked me which colour bag I wanted and how much I wanted to pay. I didn't understand why they were selling nylon bags. I said I want a nylon bag to put my shopping in. She continued asking me what kind of bag I wanted. I was really frustrated. Then I pointed to the bag I wanted. She said: Oh you mean a carrier bag! In Nigeria we call it a nylon bag.

Once I went to an agency for a job interview and I could not understand a word the woman was saying. I tried to tell her, but I couldn't understand what she was saying back! It was terrible, I was saying, I'm sorry, I can't understand what you're saying. I didn't get the job.

My accent is getting better since my children started school. They speak better English and they correct my pronunciation all the time. I try to speak to my children in Yoruba as much as I can. It's our language, the language we speak at home. They can understand Yoruba but can't speak it. I want them to speak Yoruba too, their mummy's language, their mother's language, it's more comfortable for me to speak to them in Yoruba.

I get to speak Yoruba around Swansea, I've lots of friends here who speak Yoruba, you know some of them too, X and Y you know from our group, we speak English but we speak to each other in Yoruba.

Our Children Are Our Teachers

Interview by F.Ç.

I came here as a student with my wife and son, six years ago. I could speak English, I didn't have too many problems. Just in the beginning it was difficult for me because of the accent. And the first time I went to a doctor, I wanted to say I had stomach cramps. I didn't know the word, I put my hands on my stomach and said MARORK and eventually he understood.

At first, it was difficult for me to speak English because of lack of confidence. Five years ago we were in Milton Keynes but now we are in Swansea there is more opportunity to speak English. Still, there are so many people speaking my languages, Urdu, Pashtu, Bengali, and we always speak in our own language. After some time I realised that this is not helping me. I started with my kids. When my son started nursery, I started to communicate with English people. Taking my son to nursery and back, I meet a lot of people. Now, I learn English from my children, I have 4 children now, all fluent in English. My son is the best reader in his class. Our children are our teachers. They correct our pronunciation all the time.

My wife and I speak Pashtu, my children can understand us but can't speak it. I want them to speak our language too, but English first so they can be successful. I want them to learn other languages too so they can have more opportunities.

Young Translator

Interview by F.Ç.

I have 3 brothers and 4 sisters. Some of them are in Syria, one in Turkey, one in Russia. Insh'allah they will all come here and we will live all together again.

When we came here nearly two years ago I thought I knew some English. We studied English in Syria, but English from America, not from the UK: like eggplant, not aubergine.

My teachers are nice to me. When I started, one gave me a book and said "Read!" and I couldn't. She helped me. Later another teacher asked me to read, I could read, and he said: "Good boy!"

I can speak English now. At school they can understand me. I'm only 14 but sometimes other kids make fun of me, they say I look like 40, I look like a gorilla, they tell me to go back and other swear words. I don't like it.

I want to learn other languages. I want to learn Chinese and Russian because they are beautiful languages. I can be a translator and interpreter. I translate for my mother. She can't speak English. She knows only a very few words and sentences. It can be very funny. I like helping her. She sometime uses Google Translate, she takes her phone out, she writes something in Arabic and then she calls me and she shows me the English words and she says what does this mean? How do you say that?

Being Interpreted / Becoming an Interpreter

From different interviews by F.Ç.

– *[When someone interprets for you:]* You're putting your words into someone else's mouth to say what you want to say. It doesn't give the same taste as when you would have said them…

– When you can't speak English you feel like a disabled person! You can't understand, you can't explain! If you're hungry and you need food, you can only say it like that *[miming eating food, hand to mouth]*.

Sometimes I volunteer and translate for other asylum-seekers. I do it so I can learn English, improve my English…

– My son asked me: Mom why do you not work? Why are you not going to work? I was devastated, how can I tell him that we are asylum seekers and we are not allowed to work. I then applied to work as a volunteer and I became a volunteer interpreter. I can speak five languages you know with English, and I went to university in my country so I learned some English back home. I am good at it, I can do it. Now I tell my son that I am a translator and interpreter and some days when I take him to school I tell him that I am going to work…

Job Centre: Bring Your Own Interpreter

Interview by F.Ç.

In 2015 I went to the Job Centre for the first time. I didn't understand anything they tell me. The problem was I can't understand English and my supervisor at the Job Centre is very unhappy. She tells me: "You need to bring a friend with you from your country who speaks English".

Sometimes my friend is working and he can't come. My supervisor isn't happy. She didn't help me find a job…

Come and Interpret for Us

Interview by F.Ç.

I go to the Job Centre to sign and they ask me: Do you have time for couple of hours on Wednesday to come and interpret for us?

I say: Yes.

They say they want to test me to see if I can do it. So I have an interview and they ask me some questions, then they call in another Arabic-speaking interpreter. They ask me to read something in English and then they say: Now say in Arabic exactly what that says. The interpreter checks it and says I'm good.

It was one of my friends. I laughed when I saw him. I told them he was my friend, but they just said: Fine!

Now I volunteer as an interpreter for the Job Centre, every Wednesday for two hours. They don't pay me, volunteers don't get paid. But the Job Centre gives me money, so I like working for them, as a volunteer. I've never had money and not worked for it.

They give me £73.10 a week, Job Seekers' Allowance; more than some people I know. If I was under 25, I'd get £57.90. All my money goes to the hostel where I'm staying. I don't know what would have happened to me if the Job Centre didn't give me this money. But I never had money in my life and not worked for it, so I like volunteering for the Job Centre.

I said yes because they give me money, and I've never taken money and not worked for it.

Interpreter Power

Observed by F.Ç.

The Job Centre runs English classes for beginners. One refugee helps the teacher by interpreting in class. He also conveys messages from the teacher to students outside the class. One afternoon at a drop-in, he starts a conversation with a younger man, which turns into a row. Suddenly the interpreter is shouting, louder and louder, in their language except for some repeated English phrases: "I don't care who your caseworker is!" – "Then you call her and tell her that!" – "I don't even know who your caseworker is, who is it?"

The other man is quiet and defensive. The confrontation goes round in circles until it peters out. Afterwards, asked what it had all been about, the interpreter says the Job Centre teacher asked him to tell the other man, if he sees him, to either come to the classes or let the Job Centre know. And the other man explains that he attends a different English class at that time, he didn't know he had to tell the Job Centre teacher, and he very much does not want this interpreter to talk to his caseworker at the Job Centre.

Check Pronouns

Interview by T.C.

I've been here for 3 years, I'm learning English, and by now I don't need an interpreter. They always get everything wrong. I prefer to speak for myself. They make too many mistakes. For example, in my Home Office statement, I said I'd never been to *[name of a city]*, and it was translated as I *had* been to that place. You have to check everything very carefully, because any differences in the story are a reason to refuse a claim. In my wife's statement she said she had two brothers but her solicitor wrote it down as one brother; later the Home Office said that she said different things, so they could not believe her statement.

Before you go to court, important evidence documents need to be translated. But my solicitor didn't get my documents translated in time. Just before the court hearing, he put them in Google Translate. The judge said he couldn't believe the documents: I must have written them myself. There was an important statement from a human rights organisation about my case, saying "He did this", "He did that"; but Google Translate turned it all into "*I* did this", "*I* did that". Translating the pronouns is difficult in my language. The judge was a very understanding person, luckily. He allowed me to talk to him like a human being. I was able to explain. I got my status here.

Check Prepositions

Interview by F.Ç.

H.H. is a qualified and experienced civil engineer from Darfur, Sudan. He previously worked in construction in Khartoum and in cities in the Arabian Gulf and Egypt. From 2012, for four years he volunteered as an English teacher and interpreter in the Sudanese refugee community in October 6 City, Egypt. He and his family lived there with tens of thousands of other Sudanese people, in refugee camps run by UNHCR (United Nations High Commission for Refugees), hoping to be selected for resettlement abroad. Finally his family was granted refugee status and brought to the UK for resettlement. They found themselves in Swansea. Now H.H. hopes to qualify as a professional interpreter.

While he was in the camp in Egypt, a close friend's case for resettlement was also being considered. UNHCR staff spoke English, and so did he and his friend. But whenever Sudanese refugees were interviewed, they had to speak through interpreters who spoke Egyptian Arabic – which is a very different dialect. His friend was asked what he'd been doing when he was in Sudan. He said he had worked for a contractor supplying UNAMID (the African Union / United Nations Mission in Darfur – the international peacekeeping force), in other words he had "worked with UNAMID". But the interpreter mistranslated this as "worked *for* UNAMID", and that's what was recorded in the case file.

As far as UNHCR was concerned, UNAMID employees did not need any special protection.

H.H.'s friend didn't realise the importance of the difference between "worked for" and "worked with" until it was too late. So he is still stuck in that camp in Egypt. His case for resettlement was rejected because of the interpreter's error affecting one preposition, and however much he begs UNHCR to correct this error, they refuse.

(The first time she heard this story, F.Ç. thought the friend was rejected because the interpreter had said that he had "worked for the enemy"!)

Check Assumptions

A community interpreter reports:

During one asylum hearing I attended, the applicant said he had been persecuted in his country because he was a homosexual. He was a married man. The Home Office official – speaking through an interpreter – asked his wife what she thought about his homosexuality. The interpreter gave her answer as: "I have no option, I must accept it." But what she in fact said was: "I have no objection, I accept it." The interpreter, who was from their country, was translating what he expected to hear, not what she actually said.

Check Intentions

A community interpreter reports:

Our home in Swansea is on a hill, my wife is very ill, she can't walk up and down that hill. We want to move, we went to the council. They called an interpreter on the phone, a translator. The council worker kept asking my wife to go and see her GP. My wife kept explaining that she'd already seen her GP, and the GP had written a letter. The translator kept telling the council worker that she'd *not* had a letter from her GP. I could hear that the translator wasn't saying what my wife was saying. Why would they do that?

Check Names

This story comes from a book by Katrijn Maryns: The Asylum Speaker: Language in the Belgian Asylum Procedure *(Routledge 2006, 291). She recorded asylum hearings in courts in Belgium, where both officials and asylum-speakers were speaking English (the 'common language'), without interpreters, although none of them spoke English as a first or native language (so really all speakers were 'self-interpreters').*

In the following excerpt, the official's first language is French, and she is interviewing a woman from Darfur, Sudan, whose first language is Fur, and second language, Arabic.

Official: So what happened to you in Sudan that you have to leave the country?

Asylum-seeker: Don't... When they are fighting we run...

Official: You just run away, uhum, and what happened to you, run away... so where to?

Asylum-seeker: One man... one man... carry me, help me...

Official: Karimi?

Asylum-seeker: Yeah.

Official: It was a man or a woman?

Asylum-seeker: Man.

The official misunderstood 'carry me' as a name, 'Karimi'. The asylum-seeker's answer to the question 'man or woman?' seemed to confirm the existence of this man 'Karimi'. Later on in the hearing, the asylum-seeker was asked to provide more details about this man she had mentioned. She was unable to understand these questions. The court found that her story was not credible. Her asylum claim was denied.

Are You Happy With That?

This is a 'found poem' and a mini-drama. 'Found poem': it is based on words spoken during a meeting between a solicitor in South Wales and his client, an asylum-seeker from the Democratic Republic of the Congo. The words were reported by the volunteer interpreter who was present, Sylvie Hoffmann. 'Mini-drama': Sylvie presents it so we read or hear only the voice of the solicitor, not the voices of the asylum-seeker and the interpreter. Their voices are left to our imagination. The asylum-seeker speaks French as her second or third or fourth language; her first or second language is Lingala. The interpreter speaks French and English. The solicitor speaks only English (with a Welsh accent).

At the solicitor's:
– I'm afraid we don't have an interpreter for your language.
– ... ...
– Are you happy with that?
– ... ...
– No, I'm sorry, 'I'm afraid' does not mean that I am afraid. There is nothing to fear.
– ... ...
– Are you happy with that?
– ... ...
– All communications and letters will be in English.
– ... ...
– Are you happy with that?
– ... ...
– No, I'm not asking you how you feel. 'Are you happy

with that?' simply means, 'Now, can we proceed?'
Which is not in itself a question.

– ... ...

– Are you happy with that?

– ... ...

– The Adjudicator has refused refugee status for you.

– ... ...

– Are you happy with that?

– ... ...

– You are to be evicted from your accommodation and
you face deportation.

– ... ...

– Are you happy with that?

– ... ...

– Now, this paragraph is you, sign here, and here,
thank you. You will hear from me shortly, you need
not do anything, just leave it all to me.

– ... ...

– Are you happy with that?

Fast and Slow

A professional from East Africa, who has refugee status, remembers being asked to act as an interpreter while he was an asylum-seeker. Interview by T.C.

I didn't need an interpreter for my Home Office interview, my English was already good when I got here, thanks to my education and training. My solicitor said I should have an interpreter at the hearing, because it would help me. But the judge at the hearing said: "This man needs no interpreter, he has excellent English! He has taken professional courses in this country!" He was waving his arms as he spoke. Then he apologised to my solicitor. Hastie was the judge's name, he said: "Hastie by name, hasty by nature." That was his joke. At the end of the hearing he said we would hear within a fortnight. Hastie by nature! I waited for years...

That interpreter was very good, he did his job well. Afterwards he told me that when he came to the UK, he had little English, but he got qualifications, so why didn't I do the same thing?

I did consider it. I did some interpreting a few times in the first years after I claimed asylum [in the early 2000s]. I was so full of energy back then! My solicitor asked me. She paid my expenses and a good fee. The money came in very useful. I remember there was one girl, young woman from [my country] who had been raped [in our country], before she got away to [a neighbouring country], and eventually got here. My solicitor rang me one day and asked me to go with her to see a psychiatrist in [a town about an hour away]. She gave me money for the train ticket, and afterwards she paid me £150, no, £140 pounds. *[T.C.: That was against the law, surely – you had no right to work then.]* Yes, of course. But I'd also have done it for nothing, to help, although I was glad to have the money.

So this girl, we chatted on the way, she was a nice girl, I was glad to meet her. We went through the Welsh countryside, it was a nice trip. Then we got lost in the town, the solicitor had given us a map but we got lost, but we weren't worried, someone showed us the way. We were joking and laughing. Then at the psychiatrist, she cried and cried. She cried a lot, but she had never cried before with me. Some things she said to him didn't really go together with what she had said to me before. So I knew some of it was not exactly true. Still, I translated what she said. I knew what it was for. I had no problems interpreting. Even the psychiatric terminology came easy to me. And afterwards he wrote his report, then she went to her hearing, very soon after, and with that report she got her papers very quickly, just a few weeks later.

Plenty of people have come here and got their papers very fast. I had to wait so many years for my papers...

Hearing Voices

Interview by T.C.

One time I was an interpreter, never again! Not many people speak my Kurdish language, they need translators badly. Maybe I should do it, but I was put off. I didn't have my status back then. I did it as a volunteer. I was worried my English wasn't good enough, but that wasn't the problem. I went to the psychiatric hospital. The patient was in a high security ward: that was scary for a start. He was schizophrenic, he was hearing voices in his head. So he was trying to answer the psychiatrist, but the voices kept interrupting him, and whatever the voices said, he said to us. He was interpreting them in a way. The voices were saying, he was saying, crazy things, frightening. So I was translating what he said and what the voices inside his head said, people who weren't there. People, or something, demons, I don't know. I didn't know whose voice I was hearing or whose voice I was translating. It was crazy, he was crazy, I thought I was going crazy. Can you imagine? It gave me nightmares for a long time afterwards. That was the end of my career as an interpreter.

Elected Representatives

Julie James AM (Welsh Assembly Member for Swansea West) told us that some of the constituents who come to her with problems to do with housing, education, employment, health services, etc., speak very little or no English. As an Assembly Member she has limited resources to pay for translation and interpreting to help with communication. Indeed, children as young as 5 act as interpreters at her surgeries, translating for their parents and her.

For immigration matters, Assembly Members have no powers. Asylum-seekers can ask their Member of Parliament for help. The MP can write to the Home Office to ask about the progress of a case.

Sylvie Hoffmann, acting as a volunteer interpreter for a French-speaking woman, recorded this conversation in the surgery of the late Alan Williams, MP (1930-2014):

– What does she want me to write?
– Tell him I found no solicitor to take up my case.
  Tell him where do I need to look?
  Tell him I cannot pay for one myself.
  Tell him I'm scared, my baby is babbling but I
      am scared.
– What does she want me to write?

Doctors

'Found poem' by Sylvie Hoffmann, reporting the words of a
Francophone African woman:

This GP, he won't examine me.
He examines my clothes instead,
He refuses to touch me.
He won't use LanguageLine.
He refuses to believe me.
He says I'm telling lies, he says I'm fine.
He gives me Prozac, a stronger dose each time.
It's destroying me, I cannot sleep.
They are the mad ones, not me.

Interview by F.Ç.

Ali is a refugee from Sudan. He wants to be a
policeman. He got no education in Sudan: Ali lived on
a farm, there were no schools. He goes to the doctor in
Swansea. He looks in his phone for the words he needs
to say. He hears what his doctor says, but he doesn't
understand. Ali smiles at whatever the doctor says and
says yes. He thinks it is rude not to...

Hospital

Interview by F.Ç.

I have friends from my country here *(at the drop-in)*. You come here and hear a woman talking your language, and you start talking to them. Sometimes, they translate for me and sometimes I translate for women from my country.

When I go to my GP or my solicitor, it's difficult to communicate without an interpreter. With the GP, sometimes I take a friend from my country with me. When I needed to make an appointment, I used to say I need an interpreter. The interpreter was always on the phone. One day, my GP said: Next time you come here, no translator on the phone: it's better you speak for yourself. Now I go to my GP and no interpreter. It's OK, I can tell my GP what's happening. I go there for my son, he's 2 now, he gets sick a lot.

The GP is OK. I can speak or I ask a friend to come with me. But hospitals are really difficult when you can't speak English. I had to take my son to hospital a few times. I called the emergency number and they said I must take him to hospital. I took a taxi, £14, a lot of money and then £14 back home, £28 in one night, a lot of money. Maybe, if I spoke good English, or if there was a translator on the emergency number, they would say it's OK, don't come to hospital, and I wouldn't have to pay for taxis. All my money went on taxis that week, money for food.

Translate Something Else

Interview by F.Ç.

I speak Amharic, and a little English, but I can't read and write nicely in English. When I have a letter I understand half-half, and then I go to get help with the letter in EYST: Aliya has someone to help us.

When I'm sick, I go to the GP but they don't understand my English. They call a translator on the phone, you say something and they translate something else. It's not good, but GPs don't understand my English. In my country when we learn English it's not like here.

Never Had Interpreter

Interview by F.Ç.

I am Kurdish from Iran, Kermanshah. I speak Kalhor. No one else speaks Kalhor in Swansea, only me. At Heathrow Airport, they asked me what language you speak, I said Farsi and Kurdish. They put on my Application and Registration Card: Farsi and Sorani. I can understand Sorani, I speak some Sorani, but it isn't my mother tongue. In Kermanshah, Kurds speak Kalhor, not Sorani.

I live in a shared house, there are four of us. Two of them are Kurdish, they speak Sorani. I can understand them, but not as well as English. Another is an Arabic speaker. We speak to each other in English. If you can't speak English you have a problem. You can't understand what people are saying, you can't understand what's going on. You can't even register for English classes!

I've never had official translator and interpreter helping me here. I went to the GP more than ten times, never does any translator and interpreter help me. I will go to see my GP again next week, and I will try to tell them I need a translator, because I think I have a specific problem and I don't know how to explain it to my GP.

Interpreters in the Community: More Than Language

Interviews by F.Ç.

Always Ask for LanguageLine

Zinab Khaled Battar – Asylum Health Support Worker, Swansea.

I was born in this country; I grew up multilingual. I spoke Amazigh *(also called Berber, Tamazigh)* at home with my parents, Arabic at a supplementary school in Cardiff at weekends, and English at school. I love having access to all these languages and people who speak them.

I'm from an Amazigh-speaking family, from a part of Libya where Amazigh is the native language. Our language was oppressed by Gaddafi's policy of Arabic colonisation. For decades Amazigh wasn't taught in schools or used in other institutions. Only recently, after the 2012 Libyan Revolution, they have legalised it, making it compulsory in the Amazigh towns and optional in Arab cities. It's our language and we speak it and we love it.

We went back to Libya when I was 9, for 3 years. My father came here to the UK to study medicine, he qualified as a surgeon. While he was studying he went back to Libya and married my mum and brought her here. At the time she spoke no English. My mother's uncle and his wife were also living in the UK; auntie helped my mother with everything until she learned enough English to manage on her own.

My dad got a job in Port Talbot and we settled in Baglan for a long time. Then after 10 years we moved to Libya. I was the eldest of my siblings. Language wasn't an issue: we'd travelled to Libya every summer and we spoke the languages at home and in the supplementary school. I was always excited to go to Libya. What I most like is the family and the desert.

The plan was to live there permanently but after a while it was obvious we were different, we didn't fit in.

We were taught in Arabic at school, even though we lived in an Amazigh city. Towards the end of those three years I was more fluent in Amazigh than English. My younger siblings were too young to remember any English. When we returned to Wales I experienced a culture shock. Growing up in Wales, we had our own culture at home, and living in Libya I could apply this to outside, but resettling back to Wales I was confused. I had missed years 5, 6 and 7 and it confused me a lot, I didn't know many of the subjects, but I soon settled. It was difficult for my youngest brother and sister, they started nursery and reception and they were unhappy, crying all the time because they couldn't understand any English. But in a year they learned the language like they'd always spoken English.

I studied Business Management and worked in a bank for a few months. But I wanted to do something different with my life, it didn't feel like my place. I eventually started to do translation between Arabic and English for EYST (Ethnic Youth Support Service). They really liked my style and then I became a paid translator (interpreter). Now I'm working with 7 GPs in the city of Swansea. Soon all the city centre GPs will be part of this scheme. I spend 2 hours in each GP surgery once a fortnight and see 4 clients, half an hour each. My clients are asylum-seekers; they don't know the language and the system. I work with them to show them how to get a repeat prescription or register with a dentist, or teach them that they need to ask their GP for referrals etc. During my voluntary work with EYST I learned a lot about the issues faced by asylum seekers and refugees. I attend Mental Health Forums to further familiarise myself with the issues. I met with mental health nurses and GPs and familiarised myself with the referral routes.

I listen to my clients carefully, with empathy. I always try to encourage them to be positive. Listening to them is often upsetting because their situation is so difficult. They don't know where to go, what to do, who to talk to, they can't get any answers. There are many issues related to mental health problems. Most of them already spoke to a mental health nurse and are receiving counselling or waiting to receive counselling. I refer them to African Community Centre (ACC) for one-to-one counselling and support groups. I know they can benefit from it greatly. Most of them feel lonely. ACC also pays for travel: bus tickets are a big barrier for most asylum-seekers.

Our conversations are usually in English but when language is a barrier I either take a volunteer from EYST with me or use LanguageLine – the phone interpreting service. EYST is extremely helpful and supportive. I ask all patients to ask for LanguageLine when they make an appointment. LanguageLine should always be used at GP surgeries – the NHS Trust pays for it to be available for anyone who needs it. But asylum-seekers don't even know that such a thing exists, unless someone tells them.

It's been reported to me that patients sometimes ask for LanguageLine and doctors refuse, saying the patient can speak English, or should speak English. These patients only speak 2 or 3 words. What happens is they just agree with anything the doctor says, because they don't know how to express themselves. Many doctors do try to use the service and patients show satisfaction with the service when used.

Some patients say that they use Google Translate on their mobiles. This isn't right, they should access LanguageLine. It doesn't cost the surgery. The problem is, it's difficult to arrange. It can take 2 or 3 weeks to arrange for an interpreter on the phone, and then they may cancel at the last moment. Or the patient may not turn up. Also, a GP appointment is usually for 10 minutes, but when you have someone translating on the phone, that becomes 20 minutes, which costs the surgery in terms of the GP's time.

Language is still a big issue in many ways.

In my role I try to show people how the system works and how to navigate their way around it. It's often difficult not to be affected by their stories. I find some comfort in knowing that at least I can assist them. I try to separate my work from my personal life. And I keep in mind that I'm not there to feel upset for them, or sorry for them, but to be resourceful, to help them.

The Firefly

Mr Muhammad Tahir, from Pakistan, has a Masters degree in English Literature. He often helps people with language problems. He also regularly attends the Men's Support Group at the African Community Centre in Swansea. At one meeting, he shared this poem by Allama Muhammad Iqbal (1877-1938):

ہمدردی

سنی پہ کسی شجر کی ٹہنی پہ بلبل کہتا تھا کوئی اداس بیٹھا

کہتا تھا کہ رات سر پہ آئی اُڑنے نے چٹکنے میں دن گزارا

پہنچوں کس طرح آشیاں تک ہر چیز پہ چھا گیا اندھیرا

سن کر بلبل کی آہ و زاری جگنو کوئی پاس ہی سے بولا

حاضر ہوں مدد کو جان و دل سے کیڑا ہوں مگر چمک ہے مجھ سا

کیا غم ہے جو رات ہے اندھیری میں راہ میں روشنی کروں گا

اللہ نے دی ہے مجھ کو مشعل چمکنے کے مجھے دیا بنایا

ہیں لوگ وہی جہاں میں اچھے
آتے ہیں جو کام دوسروں کے

This is an English translation, followed by Mr Tahir's comments:

> Perched on a lonely branch of a tree
> Was a nightingale, in misery,
> Lamenting at the fall of night:
> "Oh! I spent my day in carefree flight,
> But now I'm lost! Where is my nest?
> Where in the darkness can I find rest?"
> Hearing the nightingale's sorry cry
> Was a tiny, feeble firefly:
> "I'm here to help in your hour of need,
> Though I'm just a little bug. Indeed,
> The night is dark, but have no fear:
> I'll shine to show your way from here;
> Allah gave me a burning light
> To find a path in deepest night.
> Good people everywhere assist,
> With their gifts, others in their midst."

The message of the poem is: It doesn't matter how big or strong or beautiful you are, what matters is what you have to offer anybody at the hour of their need.

At primary school, I was bullied. My parents said: look at the difference of size, vitality and muscular power between the nightingale and the firefly. Yet the nightingale is lost without the firefly showing it the way. So follow the role of the firefly: become a guide for the public at large. This inspired me to pay attention to my education. I studied literature, up to Master's level. I studied the philosophical perspective of Iqbal in his poetry, among other subjects. My

English is fluent. People often ask me to help them with English documents or when they have legal issues with their cases. God gifted me to guide my fellow people in many ways.

I've been here for several years, as an asylum-seeker. I'm needed to help people with translation and interpreting a lot. As an interpreter you get into the stories of people. I'm an emotional person, I often become sad about these stories.

Sometimes I interpret over the phone, but I prefer not to, because the person being interpreted for feels more comfortable in the presence of an interpreter.

One lady I helped had initially come to the UK to join her husband. Then she divorced her husband. He had mistreated her, given her intoxicants and sedatives. The case went to the court but she was threatened with deportation. She told me what had happened, we had conversations in [two Asian languages], and I wrote up what she had said as her statement for the Immigration Tribunal. Her solicitor had given up, saying her story was not strong enough. They didn't believe the case could be won. She was desperate, no English language skills, nobody to help. I translated, I wrote her statement, and she won her case. Perhaps the solicitor didn't give her a chance because the interpreter couldn't convey her message to the solicitor. She was distressed, distraught, and helpless. I guided her out of her difficulties simply by translating and interpreting for her. It's so much more than language...!

Cross-cultural Understanding

The interviewee came to the UK from Pakistan in 1968 and settled here, marrying a Welsh woman. He is a retired gynaecologist. He remembered the time a young Pakistani woman came to the hospital accompanied by four female relatives, all in burkas. They told him the young woman was in dreadful, chronic pain and was dropping out of the university because of it. They suspected she had a urinary tract infection. She was studying to be a midwife, but she had become very depressed and just stayed at home, because of the pain.

He felt he needed to see the patient on her own, and eventually he persuaded the relatives to leave her alone with him. He is sure that it was only because he spoke their language, and understood their culture so well, that he was able to persuade them.

She confided that she was in love with a white boy from the university. "Tears were flooding her face; I held her hand and my eyes were filled with tears too. I said to her, 'You can overcome this, this isn't your destiny, you can decide for yourself'. She kept on crying, I don't know for how long. Then she stood up, and she said: 'I am going back to university.' And then she handed me back the prescription for antibiotics I had written, saying: 'I don't need that'."

Stacks of Forms

Mine Berak Evans is a Turkish/English community interpreter and Bilingual Classroom Support Worker with EMLAS, Ethnic Minority language and Achievement Service (now Ethnic Minority Achievement Unit). Interview by F.Ç.

I first came to Swansea in 1996 and it was a massive disappointment. I'd met my husband in Turkey and came to Swansea for a month. Swansea wasn't a city, it was a village. But we got married and I came to live in Swansea.

I didn't struggle with English then. In fact my English was much better then than it is now! *(She laughs.)* I think I found it difficult to understand the accent, but over time I got better.

For the first three years here, I thought I was the only Turk in Swansea. Then one day I went to a GP's surgery and I heard this woman trying to explain something to the receptionist, but talking in Turkish. So I started talking to her. She asked me to go in with her when she was called. She said they call an interpreter over the phone, but she could never manage to say what she needs to. So I went in with her and translated. That's how I started to translate and interpret.

From that moment on, all these Turkish-speaking people kept finding me. I realised there were so many people from Turkey living in Swansea. *(In 2000, the Home Office began 'dispersing' asylum-seekers from South East England to various towns and cities, including*

Swansea.) Some of them were from really rural areas, very underprivileged backgrounds; they had no knowledge of English.

I started as a translator, an interpreter on a voluntary basis. People contacted me with letters to read, forms to fill in, GPs to visit. I just found myself doing this job. I never charged, and they didn't have much to give me anyway, but they offered.

The more I translated and interpreted, the more I became known to service providers. I registered with a translation agency, and started getting paid work. I started getting calls from the NHS for hospital appointments or to accompany midwives to people's homes. There were lots of pregnancies back then, lots of babies and toddlers.

A bit later, I started working for Swansea Council, for EMLAS, going to schools. A friend of mine was working there. It wasn't a difficult application process: a simple English competence test and an interview.

The children were amazing, but I was often disappointed and frustrated with the parents. The children were mostly Kurdish, from under-privileged backgrounds, though not all were asylum seekers and refugees. Usually, neither dads nor mums could speak much English. In most cases mums' English was even worse. They were unable to help and support their children. In some cases it was pure neglect, they didn't even bring their children to school regularly or on time.

I worked with children of all ages, nursery to sixth form. I helped with lessons, communication with teachers, and schools' communication with parents.

Not every child got support, only those whose English was so bad they couldn't understand their lessons. The support could be just an hour or half a day each week. I worked for several schools.

I'd go to a school and the parents would be there with so many letters they needed translating – Home Office, solicitors, bills and so on – I'd end up with no time to go into the classroom to help the children. Often, parents would come to school meetings bringing a stack of forms that needed to be filled in. Looking back, I don't know how I managed, but I helped them a lot. I sacrificed my own time, my children's time. It was very difficult.

I remember one kid who spoke no English, 6 years old, he was really aggressive and used to beat up teachers. He'd run out of the classroom into the garden and scream like he'd never stop. He was frustrated, he didn't understand anything, and he was violent. He was expelled from four different schools. He was a danger. I don't know what happened to him later. It was heart-breaking.

What I struggled with the most was not being able to understand the parents' Turkish. I could understand words, but the sentences didn't make sense. I had to keep asking what they meant. It was absolutely horrendous, me constantly saying: "Anlamadim, tekrar soyler misiniz? Pardon, ne demek istediniz?" (I don't understand, could you repeat that? Pardon, what did you mean?)

Language – Culture – Politics

Cem Tolga Yıldız was a Bilingual Classroom Support Worker in Swansea for 2 years, working for Ethnic Minority Language and Achievement Service (EMLAS). He continues to do unpaid translating and interpreting for Turkish-speaking people in Swansea. Cem is also a musician, playing the bağlama (or saz: traditional instrument) and singing. Interview and translation by F.Ç.

I arrived in London in 2003 to study English and soon settled in Swansea. After 14 years, reminiscing feels somehow uncanny. I see so many experiences I could not envision back then. The language I came to learn has become the language I've helped many others to learn. It became the language of communication with my family, my son, my son's mother, my friends, colleagues and neighbours.

In 14 years I've seen a lot of changes in people's attitudes to migrants. In the early years in Wales I did feel welcome, people would greet me, smile at me, have conversations with me. People were curious about where I came from, about my story. My migration to here was a topic for lively conversations. Interest in my story would open the gates of friendship. I had a sense of being different and being appreciated for it.

I worked as a Bilingual Classroom Support Worker in Swansea for 2 years, from 2005. My job was to translate for children whose native language was Turkish. Pupils ranged in age from 4 to 16. I supported 26 children, most of them Kurdish. In many cases they had travelled from their home villages or towns straight to the UK; they had no previous experience of modern urban life.

One day I was called to a school to help with a 6-year-old Kurdish boy, recently arrived from Turkey. Whenever he needed to go to the toilet, this boy was going out to various spots on the edge of the school grounds and using the space as toilet. Nobody at the school could communicate with him. The teachers were frustrated. The boy was delighted to meet someone who spoke Turkish. He told me something noisy in the toilet frightened him. I eventually understood he was talking about the hand dryer. I explained what it was, took him there and showed him how to use it. His fear was resolved.

Language has many components. It's beyond the mere sound of the utterance of words. Culture is important, and culture is connected to politics. Most of the children I worked with had issues not only with the English language, but also with the Turkish language. They were from Kurdish-speaking households. In Turkey, Kurdish is not recognised as an official language: it is not used in state institutions or as a medium of education. Therefore speakers of Kurdish are not literate in Kurdish; they can't read or write in Kurdish. When they go to school, they learn Turkish. Most of the parents come from under-privileged backgrounds: they had only a few years of school education. They can read and write in Turkish, but they don't have much competence or self-confidence in that language.

Even so, the parents think it's very important to teach their children Turkish. They want to speak better Turkish themselves, and they want their children to be able speak good Turkish. It's about survival: they believe that if they speak the official language better, they'll have better chances in life. They still think like that, even though they're now living in Wales.

The mothers are the real champions: they communicate with their children and with their friends in Kurdish and in Turkish. Fathers are often more apprehensive about how well they speak Turkish.

I think you must be an expert user in one language to learn another one properly. The younger children learn English better, compared to older children: it happens quickly and naturally. Older children are often confused between Kurdish and Turkish and English. They struggle because they can't understand the logic of any languages. Without understanding how Turkish and Kurdish languages operate, they transfer patterns from those languages into English. English language acquisition is a big issue for these children.

I couldn't speak to them in my usual Turkish. I had to carefully select my words, construct my sentences and give examples so they could understand me in Turkish. If I just translated what the teacher said, I wouldn't be helping them at all. I'm not Kurdish, but I still believe I understand these children. Some of my colleagues had no understanding of these children's specific cultures.

We must also remember that these children have often had traumatic experiences. They travelled in the freight lorries, under very dangerous circumstance, then they arrived in an unknown city. Asylum-seeking families' lives are filled with uncertainty and fear. Imagine: a child would be in a maths, chemistry or physics class with me, but she'd be telling me about a letter their family had received from the Home Office the day before, how their father smoked a whole packet of cigarettes last night, their mother was crying... And these children are expected to learn English and be successful in school.

The same goes for the parents of course. They can't learn much English because they have no resources, they aren't expert users of the languages they speak, and they're stressed and desperate about their immediate future. It's a huge culture shock for many of them, coming here from rural hometowns: above all, they miss a sense of community. When they're given their visa, Leave to Remain, most move away to big cities, not for the economic opportunities or better living conditions, but for the sense of safety that comes from having a community: living close to relatives and other people that they knew before, or from the same group.

Here, the families were housed in different parts of the city, so they struggled to get together as often as they wished to. And one of the main things was food: they couldn't find the ingredients to cook the food they were used to. That has changed now. I'm still in touch with people who settled in other parts of the UK. They miss Swansea. I tell them that we now have stores that sell the ingredients they used to have to order from

London. Swansea has changed, many things have changed...

I've always thought of Wales as a friendly and welcoming place and to a large extent I still do. Have I ever experienced discrimination? No, not personally: no one has ever told me to go back to my country or been rude to me. But I've witnessed other people being subjected to it... though these episodes involved people being drunk, so I'm not sure they count.

Still, things have changed in the past 6-8 years. It's not like it used to be. I always thought that Welsh people, having the experience of being an oppressed minority themselves, were more accepting of asylum seekers, refugees and other migrants. Now I see a lot of hostility from locals to migrants, mostly to Eastern Europeans. I refuse to simplify this as discrimination by Welsh people towards migrants. Local people's perceptions are manipulated by the media. They have started to see migrants as people who changed the balance of how economic resources are being shared.

The situation has got a bit out of control since Brexit. I don't feel as welcome as I did. I feel unwanted. It's as if Brexit justified xenophobia. I'm tied to Wales, because of my love for where I live, because my son, my family is here, my life is here, but I know people are exploring their options since Brexit. I have Polish neighbours; they're now returning to Poland. It's not easy to uproot oneself but they're determined to leave the UK. Brexit divided us, here in Swansea, Brexit divided us.

Swapping Languages

This is the story of Lee Robinson, one of Cem Tolga Yıldız's school students some years ago. Lee migrated between Turkey and Wales and between Turkish and English. Interview and translation by F.Ç.

Lee is 26 and lives in Swansea, working in catering. He was born in Swansea. His father is Turkish, his mother a UK citizen originally from Malta. They spoke English at home. When Lee was 4, his father was deported to Turkey. His mother went after him with Lee, then she went back to the UK, leaving Lee with his father in Anatolia. Time passed. They lost contact with his mother. Lee grew up in Turkey with his father's family. He forgot his English and spoke only Turkish.

Lee had no official identity: no passport, no Turkish ID, no birth certificate. State education begins at age 7 in Turkey, but no school would let him enrol – until his aunt, who lived in Germany, donated money to a school and they gave him a place. But then when Lee reached the age of 11, he couldn't get a place at a secondary school. His whole existence in Turkey, living with his father and grandmother and aunts and uncles and cousins, was illegal.

Then one uncle moved to Swansea and got hold of Lee's birth certificate. Lee was able to get a UK passport. Then his father decided it would be best for him to go and live in Swansea with his uncle.

Lee said goodbye to his father at the airport, his father hugged him, Lee cried a bit. He walked towards the departure gate … and the Turkish border police detained him as an illegal. He was in detention for 5 days before his father could arrange for him to be allowed to leave Turkey. In the bus to the airport, a group of women were nice to Lee, they spoke Turkish but in a funny way. Lee didn't realise then that they were sex workers being deported from Turkey.

Lee landed at Heathrow. He asked other passengers on the flight to help him. He couldn't speak a word of English. He couldn't believe that when he was 4, English was all he could speak, but now he'd forgotten it completely. It did not seem real.

"My uncle met me at the airport and brought me to Swansea. It was June 2006. Life was different in Swansea, everything was different. I wanted to go to school but they couldn't find a school place. I stayed with my uncle for a while and didn't go to school, till he and my father and my aunt in Germany decided I should go and live with her. I spent 8 months in Germany but I couldn't enrol in school there either. I came back to Swansea. I was bit sad because I was starting to learn German and now in Swansea it was difficult because I couldn't speak English.

My uncle contacted social workers to take care of me. They were confused. They tried to send me back to Turkey because my father was there. I wanted to stay here and find my mother. They placed me in a house with older teenage boys. They were sometimes nice but sometimes mean to me. I didn't like it there. They were there because no one wanted them. I was there because no one wanted me.

The social workers gave me a book with lots of pictures, pictures of everything, under the pictures were the words, how they were written. When I wanted something I showed the pictures. I learned to read from there.

I was placed in foster care with an old couple who were really nice to me. My foster mum showed me how to use the bus, how to buy a bus ticket, which bus stop to take the bus and leave the bus. After showing me a few times she said, now you do this on your own.

I went to school but I couldn't understand anything until one day a man came and talked to me in Turkish. I was so happy. His name was Cem, I called him Cem Abi. 'Abi' is like 'big brother', he's not my big brother, and it's not like he was like a big brother to me, but we don't call people older than us by their first names, this is disrespectful, but we don't call them Mr and Mrs like here either. Cem Abi was nice. He came to my foster home to help me with my school work. But when he was in the classroom with me, I was the only one sitting there with an adult, it was embarrassing.

School was always difficult. I was bullied at school both in Turkey and here, because I look and sound foreign. It affected my confidence for such a long time.

Life has made realise how important it is to know other languages, because it changes your personality and your mentality, the way you see life and how you understand different cultures.

I don't know how long it took me to learn English but eventually Cem Abi stopped helping me. Now, I can speak English, I'm working, I've friends here, it's my community, I speak English in my community.

Türkçe konuşmaya da devam ediyorum, babamla, babaannemle, halalarımla Türkçe konuşuyorum, biliyorum İnglizce benim ana dilim, ilk sadece İngilizce konuşuyormuşum ama hatırlamıyorum. Benim hatırladığım Türkçe hep konuştum ama İnglizce öğrendim, Türkçe anadilim gibi... But I still speak Turkish too, with my father, my grandmother, my aunties. I know English is my mother tongue, I know I had been speaking only English, but I've no memory of that. What I remember is that I always spoke Turkish, and learned English, so Turkish feels like my mother tongue.

About my mother... I'll tell you another time."

Unity in Diversity: The Active Voice

Sarah Reynolds

Sarah is a student on the MA in Creative Writing at Swansea University. This report was first published as 'Yr awdur yn ei helfen: y cyflwr gweithredol', in the Welsh-language magazine O'r Pedwar Gwynt, *issue 2, Christmas 2016. Reproduced here with our thanks to the editor, Sioned Puw Rowlands.*

On a dreary Tuesday evening in Swansea, the open door of the United Reformed Church glows like an illuminated exclamation mark. Inside, a congregation of Muslims and Christians, Buddhists and agnostics has gathered together to join in a shared act of devotion. The enlightenment on offer tonight is not one of religion, but of language.

This is Unity in Diversity, a volunteer-run endeavour which aims to support Swansea's asylum seekers, providing them with social interaction, food, friendship and free English lessons. Leading the devotion is Wayne. In addition to his day job teaching English to non-native speakers, he gives up four hours of his time, twice weekly, to run this drop-in group. With his buzz cut and gap-toothed grin, he has the demeanour of an avuncular army sergeant, a useful attribute when wrangling up to seventy students.

Wayne expects everyone to get involved with the running of the evening. Whether preparing food, tidying up or making tea, the refugees who come here volunteer their time as much as Wayne and his British team. Tonight he is joined by Margaret, a spry retiree with a clipped English accent. She is keen to point out that she gets as much out of the group as anyone.

"There's no such thing as true altruism," she tells me, "We do it because it makes us feel good to help other people."

Eyeing me warily from the corner of the room is Ajay. *(All names have been changed except UiD staff.)* The only Sri Lankan here tonight, he sits alone, taciturn, confined within the glass box of his own language. He is reluctant to share his limited English with me; words have failed him before. His application for asylum was derailed over an inconsistency in his account of the events that brought him to the UK. Specifically, whether the day he escaped from detention was a Tuesday or a Thursday. When your entire case rests on the fulcrum of plausibility, the devil is in the detail.

Ajay believes there is more at play than a simple miscommunication. Where language is power, the court's interpreter is at least as important as the solicitor dealing with the case. Interpreters are fallible human beings after all, translating meaning through the prism of their own prejudice. Ajay has appealed the court's decision but if his case fails, he will be sent back to Sri Lanka to face the very authorities from which he escaped.

"I must learn English. Then I am able say what is true."

It is seven o'clock. The halal meal has been eaten and tidied away. The backgammon and draughts boards have been packed up and the students have rearranged the tables in the main hall ready to study. With limited space and only two teachers, the group is divided into 'Beginners' and 'Advanced'. Wayne leads the advanced session in the Sunday school room, while newly qualified teacher Chris prepares for the beginners' session in the main hall. As he prepares the overhead projector, his girlfriend, Pippa, offers round a pot of pens.

Eagerly seated in the front row is Hanna. She looks much older than her thirty-one years but her smile is warm and her ambition indomitable; her dream is to become a doctor. When I ask her where she comes from she gives me a list of countries: France, Turkey, Greece, Egypt, Sudan. Home was Ethiopia. Her brother is still in prison there.

"I have not words for telling what happen to me. Very bad."

The few words she has to offer create a stark picture.

"Political problem. Beating. Prison."

Her face breaks into a valiant smile.

"I don't die."

Hanna is one of the 'lucky ones' to be granted asylum in the UK, but her journey is far from over. Her new refugee status means that emergency funds and accommodation have been withdrawn; she is expected to get a job, to find a home. Hanna would like nothing more, but the English language looms before her, large as Kilimanjaro. It's the difference between a passive existence in the dole queue and the chance to become the active agent in her new life.

The lesson begins with a crucial question from Chris:
"Where can you get food in Swansea?"
Immediately, suggestions pour forth from the crowd:
"Tesco, Sainsbury's, Morrisons."
Pippa distributes a worksheet: students are required to match a Clipart picture to its corresponding label. I help Daniel complete his sheet. At twenty-four, he has travelled more in the last two years than I have travelled in my entire life. From his home in Eritrea, he walked to Ethiopia, stowed away in lorries to cross the Sahara desert, and risked drowning in the Mediterranean. He's covered some 3,500 miles to be here in this church hall, learning the names of foods he cannot afford to buy.

"What is ...?" he asks, pointing at an approximation of a pork chop. I do my best pig impersonation and he giggles like a pixie. I notice that like most of the students here tonight, he is wearing hiking trainers. With an asylum-seeker's allowance of just five pounds a day, buses are a luxury.

Next stop for me is the advanced group. I enter the Sunday school room feeling like Snow White encountering the home of the Seven Dwarves. A miniature table and eight tiny chairs take up the middle of the room. Only one of us is small enough to make use of these amenities. Wayne's 10-year-old son Lazlo sits diligently completing a grammar worksheet while twelve adults cram around the edges of the room, perched on benches and stools.

Under stuttering fluorescent lights, Wayne is explaining the passive voice. He writes on the white board: "I remember being taken to the zoo."

"Who can give me another example?" He lobs this linguistic ball out into the crowd. It is caught first by Aman, a young Eritrean man with a smile like a lemon wedge.

"I remember being interviewed in Home Office." Firoza calls out, "The criminal was jailed."

"I remember being shown my movie."
This last comes from a willowy Iranian man with sculpted sideburns and an elegantly draped scarf.

"Do you mean my movie? Or a movie?" Wayne asks, "Are you a movie star, Shahab?"
There are titters from the crowd until Shahab confirms that indeed, he is an actor – well known in Tehran. He was jailed for writing a play exploring Christianity. It is a sharp reminder of the dark subtext lurking beneath the evening's convivial banter.

It is eight o'clock and the warden is ready to lock up. Wayne packs up in a matter of moments. He tells me he's pleased with his students' progress. As he and Lazlo bundle out into the night, he calls back through the dark: "Next lesson will be even better – the Active Voice!"

PART 2

TRANSLATING PERSONAL WORDS INTO PUBLIC LANGUAGE

REFUGEE WOMEN'S POETRY

Introduction

Jeni Williams

> *A partly common language exists to which*
> *strangers can bring their own heartbeat,*
> *memories, images. A language that itself has*
> *learned from the heartbeat, memories, images of*
> *strangers.* (Adrienne Rich)

The poetry on the following pages grew out of the creative writing workshops I have held over the past 10 years (and continue to hold) with refugee women from countries as diverse as Iraq, Afghanistan, Pakistan, Iran, Lebanon, Syria, Algeria, Sudan, Kenya, Nigeria and China. Most of them were still in the process of learning English and even those who had been educated through the medium had learnt the dialects of science rather than those of poetry.

My starting point in running these workshops is that poetry is a way of developing a personal voice. After all, as poet and critic Adrienne Rich points out, 'someone writing a poem believes in a reader, in readers, of that poem'. In attempting to speak directly and immediately with those who read or listen to it, the language of poetry challenges that of the impersonal bureaucratic system which envelops the refugee from the moment of her arrival. This is an administrative non-language which loses connection to the physical and temporal being of the individual through generalisation and abstraction, and subjects the individual to complicated, often incomprehensible rules.

For those who have not encountered these rules, here is an extract from a letter from the Home Office, sent to a Jehovah's Witness, a woman who was volunteering with several organisations in Swansea:

> If you wish to work voluntarily you must seek permission from your Asylum Caseowner. You must also stop all voluntary activities such as sharing the bible message to people wherever and whenever as you stated. This is a form of voluntary work. So please seek permission before continuing.

Freedom of expression of religious belief is guaranteed by Article 9 of the Human Rights Act 2008. Yet the letter-writer arbitrarily redefines it as 'voluntary work'. Asylum-seekers are in fact banned from doing 'work', including 'voluntary work'. However, they are allowed to do 'voluntary activities'. The letter confuses the two.

When this Home Office decision was challenged, the response was as follows:

> You can get an updated clarification on the Voluntary work from your case owner, please write to them informing them that you are only 'Preaching and sharing the bible message with others as part of your belief and Worship' at your local Choice of worship which is registered establishment.

The mistakes in grammar and wording make no sense. In fact Jehovah's Witnesses from many countries claim asylum in the UK, and are granted it, on the basis that here, unlike many other countries, people are free to preach the Bible – and not only at a nonsensical 'Choice of worship which is a registered establishment'.

These extracts typify an administrative language that tries to process people by placing them in boxes, abstracting and assessing the refugee in terms of credibility or deceit. Asylum seekers can be switched from one category to another without the processor having to engage with them as individuals. The refugee is bewildered as his harrowing personal stories are discounted because he lacks 'credible evidence' and accounts of torture or persecution are dismissed because they lack 'incontrovertible proof'. Within an administrative system that denies the individual, it is only a matter of degree, not material difference, when the dehumanising language of swarms, floods, or cockroaches is used.

The refugee learns to 'speak' this narrowed language. In order to enter the asylum process, she learns to mirror its use of abstraction and its key words: suffering, persecution, oppression, human rights. This almost certainly reflects lived reality, but when expression is stripped of its sensuous particularity it loses its ability to connect with those who read or hear it.

When editing the writing from the first of the workshops I began to understand the extent to which a discourse of credibility generates specific expectations of the function and meaning of 'refugee writing'. First, unshaped, 'raw' testimony is seen as a mark of 'authentic' writing – and this lack of shape often means that the detail that enables the experience to be personal gets lost in generality. Second, the purpose of the writing is not about self-expression but about jolting the reader into action by alerting him or her to the lack of credibility of media reports. Finally, such writing must focus on trauma.

The significance of 'refugee writing', as commonly understood, thus lies in the marketing of collective suffering. Refugees are driven to 'tell their stories' by the Home Office and by the courts, by the media, and sometimes by researchers; and the stories they are expected to tell are ones that demonstrate their 'credibility', their 'genuine' need for sanctuary. They must in effect sell themselves as victims, on terms prescribed by the law and the media.

But the degraded language of administration is blind to ethical responsibilities, such as the care of the vulnerable other. The dehumanisation which began with the asylum process a few decades ago is now applied to groups such as the unemployed, the sick and disabled. Even stories that appear 'credible' have little effect on those who replicate official suspicions in their distrust of facts. The philosopher Jean Baudrillard thinks people now live in a 'state of fundamental incredulity' and points to the logical outcome of a language based on questions of credibility: 'Do people believe in information? Everyone pretends to. … But in the end, do people believe in it? I'm not so sure'.

This lack of trust, this inability to believe anything as other than an expression of self-interest, has clear and disastrous political outcomes. Baudrillard's assessment is chilling: 'People don't know what they want anymore. People are only sure what they don't want. The current processes are processes of rejection, of disaffection, of allergy'. When people see difference as threat, the processes of allergy and rejection intensify the breakdown of community and increase individual alienation. It affects all of us.

The language of poetry works in a very different way. It is not about factual truth, or message. It avoids generality and abstraction. It links unusual things. It seeks to engage its readers individually through an individual voice. This is why Adrienne Rich insists that poetry must be poetry, not information: 'I can't write a poem simply from good intentions, wanting to set things right, make it all better; the energy will leak out of it, it will end by meaning less than it says.'

Amani Bakhiet's love poem, 'The Colour of You in My Mind', translated from Arabic, demonstrates what is missing in a dry exchange of facts. Full of fluid, passionate images, rhythm and movement, it bears out Rich's analysis of poetry as a revitalising force that introduces 'an exchange of electrical currents through language – that daily, mundane, abused, and ill-prized medium'. The emotional range and sense of physical being of this poem generates an intensely personal response from readers and an acknowledgement of the extraordinary individual who wrote it.

> You magnetise me, pull me to you in the height of
> your power.
> My body, my being drawn to follow,
> all the seasons of my heart extended alive in
> glowing pulsation,
> in firepoints and explosions of light, in festival.

Between my grasp and the endlessly out of reach;
when quiet evening descends,
its calm quenched with the radiance that is you,
when rising, brimming, bubbling up,
the morning brightens with your fineness ...

For other writers, the lack of full facility with a language need not prevent them from cutting through 'that daily, mundane, abused, and ill-prized medium' to produce an electric shock of recognition of individual tragedy. In the quiet, puzzled repetitions of 'No Celebration This Year (Damascus, August 2012)', Sliva Kiki – a Syrian woman – records her 5-year-old niece's attempt, via Skype, to make sense of what is happening around her. The result is heartbreaking:

She says, *No celebration this year.*
She is five.
She is thinking about the children who go away
and don't come back.

The Writing and the Workshops

Because of my involvement with women's groups, the writing workshops I set up focused on developing women's voices. From the outset these workshops explored writing as a creative process that extended and redefined the writer, even as it told (part of) their story. We discussed how writing oneself as victim might affect a long-term sense of self, and we discussed the value of poetic structure and form in giving dignity and deliberation to the words. This structuring can be seen in Kiki's poem as much as in Hannah Sabatia's extraordinary 'Door Poems' sequence.

The poems move away from abstraction and express themselves obliquely. Maria Shafayat, for example, uses intense image and shaped sensory expression in 'There Was Nothing but Dreams':

> The day rose upon her,
> she felt nothing but the heat,
> Burnt her down to the soul.
>
> She is scared to dream again.
> Her hands are all blood
> from gathering the pieces of dreams ...

Something happens to time in these poems. Here again from Sliva Kiki's 'No Celebration This Year':

> She is thinking about the other children,
> the children hungry or in a safer place.
> She says. No celebration this year.
>
> She says, what will happen with us?
> With other people.
> With our neighbours.
> With friends.
> She is carefully thinking.

The future – as in so many of these poems – is problematized, particularly by the loss of the communal celebratory markers that give the passage of time meaning to a child. Another of Maria Shafayat's poems records the comfortable voice of a child detailing the order of her safe world:

> When I was a child

I woke up and thought

> *When is Eid gone, Eid ul Adha is coming*
> *When Eid ul Adha is gone, Rabi ul awal is coming.*

The rest of Shafayat's poem builds on this litany of lost markers to conclude in the loss of order and safety together. This loss of childhood security is particular to the writer but it is also an experience which we all recognise. As Rebecca Solnit notes: 'We are all in some senses refugees from a lost world':

> The very idea of self as an entity bounded by the borders of the skin is a fiction disguising the vast geographies [of home] contained under that skin that will never let you go.

In the next poem, time and home are still further complicated. The family of the writer, Aliya Khalil, fled first from Basra to Baghdad, then from Baghdad to Libya, returned to Baghdad after the invasion in 2003, fled chaos there, and is now scattered all over the world. Khalil does not look back to a treasured moment from the past but crucially to the night before it takes place: she imagines herself simultaneously at four years old, looking forward, and as an adult, looking back. The two timelines meet in a much-loved photograph – now lost, like all the others, in the first flight from Basra. The child delightedly plans her celebration of Eid:

> I will wear my new white dress
> and my new pink shoes –
> I put them safe under my pillow –

I will put them on first thing in the morning.
(…)
And my shoes, my new pink shoes
With their golden rings...
It seems always I dreamed of pink shoes
and this Eid the dream comes true.
I think of how my friends and neighbours will stare and
say
O Aliya is wearing pink shoes!

The adult looks back, recognising the fragility of such security:

We will cross the sky blue wooden bridge
to the park on Sinbad island.
I will be frightened as we walk over the running water
but my dad will be with me.
He will protect me, hold me safe.

Glimpses of personal stories characterise Hannah Sabatia's wonderful 'Door Poems'. The first three evoke Kenya, the next three, the asylum process, and the last, a child's experience of loneliness and disorientation and a mother's unspoken powerlessness. The reader is drawn to imagine events before and after each pared-down fragment, the gaps inviting the reader to imagine them more fully. The second group vividly illustrates the dehumanisation of an insistence on credibility:

All we need is safety
but.
Why did you lie?
threats

threats.

All we speak is taped,
taped and recorded,
one by one.

Something has happened to time here too: it stops,
loses meaning:

A long day and nothing new.
Out in the endless fields,
Long barbed spiked wire at the edge.

The morning sun a warm blanket.

We take photographs of our long shadows,
they are metres long.
A long day, a long, long day.

Memories of nothing.

Educated in English, Sabatia is able to work directly
with the intonations of the language, creating an
assured and utterly distinctive voice.

Of course not every woman attending these sessions
had the same level of English and not all of the poems
could be as carefully crafted. In some sessions women
had good English skills and workshops were run
almost entirely in English with little need for
interpretation. Attention could be focused on the kind
of English used – imaginative and concrete, with
attention to rhythm and structure – and the results are
impressive. However, an unforeseen effect of the
increased communication enabled by social media
meant that women with no or very little English began

to turn up to the sessions, having been told about the workshops by community interpreters. For these women, individualised attention to vocabulary, detail and structure was impossible. One of the results was that the creative expression is less sophisticated, but their focus on the individual memory remains vitally poignant. Ayun Ahmed sees a teapot in the museum and writes of her memories of her mother in Somalia:

When I saw, it remind me of back home
when my mother cook a tea for us.
Waking up early morning,
when I smell the boiling tea it waking me up –
feeling so happy.
Beautiful morning start.

Kaiyun He, far from China, considers other people's lives. She remembers anonymous travellers speeding past her on an early morning train –

I didn't know who was sitting behind the window.
I didn't know what they were doing.
I didn't know what did they think about at that time.

– and she sees a picture of 'a simple valley life' in Wales and recalls her grandparents. Saba Humayun's memory of catching fire as a child in Pakistan is terrifying in its blank shock:

My mum look at me and I was covered with, full of, fire.
And the fire came to my hair as well.
It burnt half its length.

These small narratives offer glimpses of individual inner worlds that challenge any crude assessment of 'credibility' as a means of determining the value of a human life.

At times, however, the mixture of languages and lack of English as a common bridge led to difficulties that interpretation could not resolve. It was a question of balance. One example stands out – a Pashtun woman from Afghanistan, who had learnt Punjabi as a second language while a refugee in Pakistan, was able to communicate with an Urdu speaker who then translated her words into limited English. However, because the Urdu speaker could not understand her Punjabi script, the transmission was fragmented. She had to read her text aloud for it to be translated via Urdu into English. Expression was reduced to an attempt to convey the events of traumatic experiences and all nuance and detail disappeared. With so many barriers, the individual gets lost in translation, and my fear was that the woman would be returned to the traumatic event without resolving anything. Meanwhile, in the same session were some Chinese women who could not speak English, and speakers of other languages with restricted English. I had to find a new strategy.

I decided to run a group in which all members spoke the same language. The idea was that there would only be one language to bridge and so I could work with all of them, with a minimum of one interpreter – more if possible. The session I ran was Chinese only. There were 13 women, only one of whom had (limited) functional English. This did restrict what we did – I tried riddles and stories, and we laughed a lot, but there were additional unexpected problems. I had not realised that all of the women would have a home language as well as Mandarin. Several used a simplified script and seemed reluctant to show their writing to others. A Chinese Malay who only had a few ideograms gave up. However, the whole experience was a fascinating example of local community interpreting. (The cover image of this book carries some writing and translating notes from this workshop.) As more women attend the workshops with poor, often extremely poor, English, and as the women became involved in layers of complicated interpreting, the workshops have had to change in response to the new situation.

The value of this activity for a sense of integration and understanding, especially for women with more advanced or fluent English, can be seen in an extraordinary poem written by Grace Omoloso. Omoloso was sold to labour at 5 and trafficked to Britain at 14. She chose not to write of FGM, beating and abuse in Nigeria, nor about the miscarriage of three babies in Britain (the last due to criminal neglect of her health and welfare in Yarlswood Detention Centre). She decided she didn't want to think about herself in this way and chose instead to write about being a child worker of 6 or 7, throwing stones to knock ripe mangoes from a tree:

> The people come out shouting
> 'You people from the second village…'
> Our stones hit their houses, break their cooking pots.
> (…)

We are deaf to everything, we cannot stop.
We look up, watch where the stones go,
see who hits which fruit, dodge the stones coming down
Everything is invisible, everything is unreal except the
mango tree.

For her, there is no lost safety which must be mourned.
Instead time occurs in moments of pleasure snatched
from an arc of suffering which is accepted but not
allowed to dominate:

I know some will be beaten by the villages –
but that can wait.
I know I will be shouted at –
but that can wait.
I don't think about pain
even though I was beaten yesterday.

The choice of this memory above all the tragedy
conveys her determination and resilience:

Whatever I do when I am at home I am always in trouble.
There is no place for me. But when I am eating mangoes,
when I am walking that hot way through the stream,
it's like I'm flying.
This is the place I can show myself, not be shy nor quiet,
this is my space, where I can let myself loose.

And I'm not alone there.
Even though the neighbours chase us with canes we
                              are free,
Brave, ourselves in our own space,
not obedient, not how those who work us,
who beat us and train us, not how they think
we are.

This poem enables us to think beyond the clichés of either media pariah *or* pitied victim – in her words 'we are free, … not how they think / we are'.

The title of this collection, *My Heart Loves in My Language*, is taken from Hannah Sabatia's poem 'The Sound of My Language'. For her the key is the creativity and expression that it enables:

I'm proud of my language
I know exactly what I mean
I can expound in it
I can tell in it
I can discuss in it.
It sounds so clear in my language
It is my mother's tongue.

My heart loves in my language,
I can love in it.
I can dream in it.
I can shout in it.

The function of the workshops is to develop a personal voice in English as a language in which speakers can express themselves more fully and in which the heart can love. This being the case, these poems bear out Rich's point that the communication of poetry is only possible because 'a partly common language exists to which strangers can bring their own heartbeat, memories, images. A language that itself has learned from the heartbeat, memories, images of strangers.'[1]

---

[1] Adrienne Rich, 'Someone is Writing a Poem' (1993). The essay can be read on poetryfoundation.org.

The Colour of You in My Mind

because you are the starting point,
the threshold
 of a purer clearer world.

What drives me to you is the magnificent intensity of
speech.
Such elation.
   So, suspended,
      depending on you,
         giving myself up to the moment,
            to life coming up,
and the moment stands still.
I just lean and
stop.

You magnetise me, pull me to you in the height of your
                  power.
My body, my being drawn to follow,
all the seasons of my heart extended alive in glowing
                  pulsation,
in firepoints and explosions of light, in festival.

Between my grasp and the endlessly out of reach:
when quiet evening descends
its calm quenched with the radiance that is you,
when rising, brimming, bubbling up,
the morning brightens with your fineness,

I give you freely my promise that
      my self will meet your self

I offer my sweetness, my spontaneity to that whole,
breaching the line that marks the separation of my
being and the sky
So that life springs up between us.
Love as the crown of our life together and its sceptre.

You are wrapped with my heart's warmth, you are
filled with my love,
the expansion and season of delight, the joy of desire.

I am giving you the sun of my celebration, my hot
longing,
the whisper of my heart's pulse,
my deep truth.
Chosen one
the place I belong is with you,
opening my heart's secrets
in the space of revelation.

Amani Bakhiet (Sudan)
Translated by Jeni Williams with the author

A Tea Bottle in the Museum

When I saw, it remind me of back home
when my mother cook a tea for us.
Waking up early morning,
when I smell the boiling tea it waking me up –
feeling so happy.
Beautiful morning start.

Getting up, looking my mam, kiss her laughing.
So happy. We eat our breakfast bread and egg
And getting ready to go school.
I get my books, my mum give me money
I can buy something at breaktime at school.

I wish that days come back to feel happy and safe.
I wish times going back to live again with my family
I wish to hug my mam and sleep in her arms.
If time can go back I wish see my mam,
never leave her again.

I wish I can speak with her
I wish my mam was alive.
I need to talk her.
I feel empty without her
I need to talk her.

Ayun Ahmed (Somalia)

Boxes

Inside the box I see one child frightened from people
Who threaten her, abuse her family, try to abduct her.
Her life is being isolated every time.
A five year girl suffer all the time but
she is still happy she knows things will change but
time by time the consequences getting worse and
                    worse.

Now she feel hopeless, exhausted.
Tried to kill herself
But God want her to be alive and accept all the
                    challenges
How she is being through.

Inside the box she left her home country
She left her relatives, father,
Ran away from her country
She came to the new country to save her life.
She relaxes but is scared about the past
Her past is not letting her alone,
Surrounded her all the time.

She suffering.
She still pretend to be happy
Because she don't want to show to other people.

Inside the box she see that her father left her.

Saba Humayun (Pakistan)

Childhood in Karachi

When I was a child
I woke up and thought

When is Eid gone, Eid ul Adha is coming
When Eid ul Adha is gone, Rabi ul awal is coming.

I woke up and thought
on Sunday
I will go with dad to the market
and we will buy mangoes.

I used to think that
on 1st of the month
I will go with mommy to the grocers
and she will buy me jellies

I used to think of
reading stories all the long summer afternoons.

When playing in the rain,
I used to shout to the sky *more rain! more rain !*
When playing on the beach
I used to wait for the big tides
to wash off all the sand under my feet and tickle me

I used to keep my pocket money to buy nail polish,
novels.
I used to wait for my brother and
we would go to the other block of housing
and buy new story books from the hawkers
I used to go to weddings just to look at the brides

and to run around the hall.

I used to play in our garden
counting and naming the coconut trees or digging in
the sand,
And all of us would spray each other with the water
hose
and scream and run around laughing.

When I was a child there was order
And I was safe.

Maria Shafayat (Pakistan)

Curious

I am very curious about you.
You have lived eight decades going to nine,
I am curious to find your secret.

You still hold a big smile on your face.
I have seen your back become bent,
I have seen your teeth fall,
I have seen your face shrink,
I have seen your skin sag,
I have seen you grow short.
And I am very curious about you.

You have witnessed one war as a girl.
How did you survive I wonder.
You have talked about your life in the mission,
Eating with white men,
Learning to eat with fork and knife.
How you laughed when the steak
Slid off your plate as you
Tried to copy the new manners.
How your friend ran away from home
Against parents' wishes
Just to learn to read and write.
I am very curious about you.

Now I see your step-children
Look down on you.
I see them try to bring you down,
Abuse you, call you names.
I have seen misery brought to you.

But I still haven't seen your downside.
I am very curious about you.

Hannah Sabatia (Kenya)

Garbage

She says,
　'I am garbage of no use
　You can recycle the trash
　But I feel a piece of junk
　Who cannot be recycled.'

She says,
　'When they talk about me
　I feel I am part of land fill
　Full of dirt and useless items of mankind
　Unwanted weight on the heart of world!'

She says,
　'I feel the same; unwanted and useless
　I hear the sounds
　All the time
　Which yell, shout and scream at me.'

She says,
　'My body is all bruised outside and within,
　I can see the lips moving
　But my hearing is so numb
　Sounds are spinning in my head,'

She says,
　'My eyes are reviewing the scenes
　And harsh, shrill sounds envelope me
　I feel no mercy from once loved ones
　I wonder why I bother.'

She says,
   'If he thinks I am piece of junk
   Why does he matter to me?
   Why do I let him hurt me?
   Why do I let him hurt my soul and my body?'

Maria Shafayat (Pakistan)

I am Syria

(2012)

I am Syria
Exiled in and out of my homeland
I am Syria
Sunni, Shiite and Durzi

I am Syria
Christian and Alawii
I am Syria
Kurd and Circassian
Syria is my land
Syria is my identity

My scent of my home land is jasmine and rose
I am son of this land
Rich with olives
Rich with apples and figs
I am son of that paradise

How many harvest is hunger and thirst
 Blood every where
 Broken every where
 Sadness every where
 Hunger every where

4 million Syrians on the border
9 million Syrians in hunger
3 million Syrians refugees

Sliva Kiki (Syria)

Life in the Future

It's a beautiful life in the future
My house without a door –
for why would I need one?
Just a roof over my head
In the future, the burglars will be farmers
whose wheat I will bake into warm fresh bread

in the future my neighbour
will be my neighbour.
One language, one colour of
Skin, one country of the world
This is my life in the future.

Life in the future: I will not text you
I will come to sit under the Muguno tree
To chat and listen - as long as you like -
With a calabash of uji and happiness.
It will smell of fruit, all the blossoms,
Roses, lavender and a fragrance like the spices
                of Lebanon.

Hannah Sabatia (Kenya)

Lost

When I walk down that familiar street I feel that it is
somewhere
That is close to me but I can't see it because I lost it.
But I can feel it, the place is reminding me
It is where I begin my life
Every moment, every day I remember the smells and
the crowds of people
I miss my grandfather
I feel emotionally suffocated.
But I need to find out what I lost.

Once upon a time when I was a child I was sitting with
my family at night
Suddenly the light had shut down, I stood up to light
the candle
Then I went to my outside door to lock it,
My little sister behind me holding the candle
The fire came to my dress and became bigger
I shout for help but my mother thinks I am fighting
with my sister
I scream a lot but nobody comes to help me
Then I ran away quickly to the room
My mum look at me and I was covered with, full of,
fire
And the fire came to my hair as well.
It burnt half its length.
She started to cry – she didn't know how to put off the
fire
Then she laid me down on the floor to put off the fire

with her hand
By the time when she put off the fire
My all dress back was burnt and my back
The skin was fully burnt and my hair as well.

Saba Humayun (Pakistan)

My Pretty Pink Shoes

I introduce you to my pretty pink shoes
My pair that just fits me

They are flat and easy to walk in
A pink pair easy to see
My pair that just fits me

You want them but you can't have them
Pink to make you wink
Or to make you think.
… because they just fit me!

I don't know your colour but I do know mine
And mine just suits me
Pink is hard to hide
And this pair just fit me.

You see I don't think they fit you
I can walk places in my pink, pretty shoes
With a smile on my face and I can dance
Because my pair just fit me.

I don't know your size
but I don't care
I do know mine
And my shoes just fit me fine

Hannah Sabatia (Kenya)

My Sister Hamdi

I miss her singing
In the morning and afternoon
My sister Hamdi
My heart is pumping
Wadnaha ayaa i dhag leh

I miss her singing
She has a strong voice
She is shorter than me,
She is smarter than me a lot.
She can discover new worlds
She writes poetry
She writes about how she feels
She makes poetry about people and houses.
My sister Hamdi

I miss her singing
My heart is pumping
My sister she is pretty, she has big, smiling eyes
She wears a blue dirac
A light blue
Like this pen I hold

My sister Hamdi
I can see her in my mind
Sitting on the rug and putting
Her mask of turmeric on her face.
Wearing her old black dress
It is a small room with yellow walls
And the carpet's colour is yellow and dark blue.

It is a warm room and she is opening the window.
She is burning her uunsi to make
Nice smells.

She is at home and I am here
I miss my sister a lot

Asiya Warsama Osman (Somalia)

No Celebration This Year

(Damascus, August 2012)

She says, *No celebration this year.*

She is five.
She is thinking about the children who go away
and don't come back.
She is thinking about the other children,
the children hungry or in a safer place.

She says, *No celebration this year.*

She says, What will happen with us?
With other people.
With our neighbours.
With friends.

She is carefully thinking.
She is carefully thinking.

She says, *No celebration this year.*
She is thinking.
She asks her nani.
She wants to stay at her house.
Her own house is too much high.
She hears the tank sound and the plane sound.

She says, What will happen with us?
She says, What will happen with us?

She is waiting until everything is finished

Before she goes outside with her friends to play
Her favourite game.
She is carefully thinking.

Sliva Kiki (Syria)

Painting

When I first
looked
at this painting

I was sucked into its heart.
It held me firm.

This painting

that depicts a girl's loose hair
hanging down her back.

Petals of sunlight
dapple a delicate waterfall
of soft waves.

An astonishing image.
Intensely quiet.

The girl pure as an angel.

It has so much beauty

that I can't help but imagine
the face I cannot see.

And I know in my heart that she is
extraordinary –
a truly beautiful girl

Xuecheng Cai (China)
translated by Jeni Williams & Duo Luan

Something Lost

I used to have a lot of confidence when I was young
but not any more.
And I used to like art when I was young
but slowly, slowly it is gone.

I used to like painting
in thick colours together,
olive green and gold yellow,
like flowers and animals.
I like horses and I used to like draw pictures of lions

I can't do this now but
when I was seven and six,
when I was a naughty little girl,
I used to mess my clothes
and my mom sometimes
Used to be angry.

Asiya Warsama Osman (Somalia)

Syria, My Lovely Country

Syria my lovely country
How can I forget you?
How can I forget your children?
How can I forget your young and your old people?

Syria my lovely country
How can I forget your sky, your sea, your flowers
Your jasmine, your roses
Your schools, your universities.

Syria, my lovely country:
Destroyed: all your dreams.
Destroyed: all your histories.
Burned: all your houses.
Burned: all your churches, your mosques.
Your children orphaned.
Your wives displaced.

Syria my lovely country:
You have become a piece of ash.
In every house a martyr.
Oh my paradise –
How can I forget you?

We will be back one day to wipe the tears on your
cheeks
We will be back to rebuild you
your schools, your universities,
your houses, your churches, your mosques.

We will be back to pray for the martyrs

My lovely Syria
You are in my heart

Sliva Kiki (Syria)

Take the Map

Take the map
And arrange it as you want
The continents are you
And I am you

From your name, the geography
of the place begins
And from your eyes, the seas
take their colours
And from your mouth shall be
born day and night
And from the rhythms of your
voice and from the veins of your
hands I am born

Your love is chasing me
As a shark which does not
feel full
It's chasing me over and under
the water
It's choosing the weakness in
my femininity
And hitting me without stopping
Hitting me on my face
Hitting me on my chest
Hitting me on my fingers
So that my blood is dyeing
all oceans in the red
colour

Daad Lubeck (Syria)

The Home I Used to Live

The town of home I used to live was very poor but was
full of love.
The home I used to live was very small but we don't
feel it small
because all our family was together, enjoying,
laughing.
I never think about what will happen tomorrow,
everything was nice and peaceful.
When I see children playing I remember my childhood
when I was playing with my friend.
I really miss that.

When I walk down the street I see the houses, and
children playing.
There are trees and stones on that street.
The smell is fresh baking of bread and the house
colours are red and white.
When I walk down the street I see the river where I
used to play when I was a child.
When it rains the river sometimes is very full
it pours over the street and washes houses away.

When the fire came in our room I ran away without
telling my family.
I was wearing a short dress and my hair was very
messy.
I wasn't wearing shoes. I just ran away.

I went very far. I stayed in the middle of the road for
two hours.

I was looking to see if someone is running looking for
     me.
But no one was coming.
All people was normal, just walking.

And I decided to go back home to find my family.
They were looking for me, my mother, my brother, my
     grandmother.
My mum was crying. She was thinking I was lost.
And the fire wasn't there anymore.
It just burnt our room but it didn't damage everything.

I miss everything, especially my family.
I feel sad and lost.

I used to like very sad music but everything was good.
So now I think it is my fault what happened in my life
     because of what I was listening to before.

After I arrive in Swansea I close everything in my heart
     just to live.

Ayun Ahmed (Somalia)

The Moon

It shone too close tonight
Golden and orange circle
Made my body shiver
Huge, on clear skies,
Even dark clouds cannot contain it
If I can touch it,
I can smell it
I wonder if it's hot or cold.

It was like this the night I met him
Years before that last slap
He promised me the moon

But...

Tonight I understand
Tonight I see so clearly
It's beautiful

Now there will be no more listening to fables
The moon is stationed in its immovable place

Hannah Sabatia (Kenya)

The Old Photograph

It was a very long time ago
The man wearing hat and long coat.
The man look very poor.
There is a woman walking on the road.
She is wearing long black coat and head scarf.
The other man look rich.
He stop the man to pay something –
he has an old cart selling food

The weather look very cold.
The sky is grey.
The time looks very early morning.

When I saw the cart I remember my country.
We used to have this cart with donkey.
They used to sell milk and water.
We really was very poor – we don't have water at
home.
We use to wait the donkey cart for water,
wait until it come pass in our road

Ayun Ahmed (Somalia)

The Photograph

Tomorrow is Eid.
I can't wait till tomorrow.
I wish tomorrow comes quickly.
I wish tomorrow comes now.
Then I will wear my new white dress
and my new pink shoes –
I put them safe under my pillow –
I will put them on first thing in the morning.

The dress is white
leaves of green threads are embroidered all round the
                    skirt
and over the front.
It is so beautiful!
It sticks out from the waist and
there is a net lining.
It was made with the soul.

And my shoes, my new pink shoes
With their golden rings...
It seems always I dreamed of pink shoes
and this Eid the dream comes true.
I think of how my friends and neighbours will stare
                    and say
O Aliya is wearing pink shoes!

I can't wait till tomorrow:
everywhere the smell of cake and woodsmoke.
I will eat the small Eid cakes
my grandmother bakes

in the clay oven in our garden,
each one carefully stuck to the sides.

I can't wait till tomorrow:
I will kiss my grandmother, kiss my Mum and Dad
Everyone, everyone will give me *Eideat*
I will be so happy with so much money.

I can't wait till tomorrow:
my dad will take me to the most beautiful place I have
ever seen.
We will cross the sky blue wooden bridge to
the park on Sinbad island.
I will be frightened as we walk over the running water
But my dad will be with me.
He will protect me, hold me safe.

And in the sun I'll walk over the pool on the white
stepping stones
To get to the fountain in the middle
And my new dress will get wet with water drops
But my mum will not shout at me
There will be many children there with their mums
and dads
And I will be so proud and happy with my dad and
my sisters
And my pink shoes.

My Dad will ask the man with the camera to take our
photograph
where we stand near the fountain.
Me and my sister will stand in the front

and my handsome dad in his white shirt and black
      trousers
with his watch with its big square face shining
will hold my little sister at the back

Aliya Khalil (Iraq)

The Picture in the Museum

It's a picture that shows the simple valley life.

A woman holds a baby and stands next to a man.
A little girl feeds the chickens
A woman who is a little bit old,
 Maybe she is the girl's grandmom.
She stands behind the girl and watch her,
She is smiley.

At left, a woman hang over a sheet under the sun.
At the right of picture, there are three old people.
One man sit on the bench and read newspaper.
An old woman just sit quiet next to him.
A man sit on the stone lay on the wall with a pipe.
It's a very peaceful and lovely valley.

I lived in a town, my parents ran a small business.
But my grandparents were farmers like this.

Kaiyun He (China)

The Sound of My Language

It is so smooth when I speak it
When I sound it
Do you understand it?
It is the sound of my language.

I can say it well in my language
It sound so nice in my language
I can understand it
I can explain it
I can sound it
It is my language

I'm proud of my language
I know exactly what I mean
I can expound in it
I can tell in it
I can discuss in it.
It sounds so clear in my language
It is my mother's tongue.

My heart loves in my language
I can love in it.
I can dream in it.
I can shout in it.

But I can't translate it
So it sounds like my language.

Hannah Sabatia (Kenya)

The Taste of Mangoes

When I'm sleeping I dream
of the mango tree in season
and dream of tasting the mangoes.

Mango trees are three people tall,
trunks I can put my arms round,
spreading branches with small leaves, dark green,
         shining,
beautiful in the sunlight.

I am thinking of a particular mango tree
that grows in the middle of a village,
stands there on its own,
houses on the left and right and a space all round.
The women take their chairs and sit quiet in its shade.

This is not my village.
It is the second village.
My friends and I walk over the hot dry hill,
through the trees and into the cool stream,
tiny fish, silver, flat ones and thin ones,
catfish black and darting away from my toes.

I am small, 6 or 7, I awake early.
I want the morning to come quickly
because then the afternoon will come.

In the morning I work on the farm,
gathering produce to sell in both villages.
But I don't care about these things, I want

to run to the next village and taste the mango.

My village is the biggest.
We have 50 round huts, each with two rooms and palm
           leaf roofs;
just 30 huts in the other village.
They are made with mud and sand so coarse that if
           your back itches
you can stand and scratch it on the rough red walls.

There are no mangoes in my village.
But in the next village the mango tree stands higher
           than the huts.
I can see it shining in the sun as I get close.
The smell of fruit is rising in the heat.

It is hot, very hot.
We balance our metal trays on our heads,
the vegetables in portions separated with small sticks,
walking in the sun over the hard hot soil until
we hear the sound of the stream trickling over rocks.

Now I am walking through trees full of the sound of
           birds singing,
When I put my feet in the stream I feel
I am peaceful, in heaven.
The motion of the water runs through my body.
I lay my tray down, wash my hands and face.
It calms me, calms me down.

I am walking from the first village with my friends,
Sometimes four of us, sometimes more,

all 6 or 7 years, girls and boys.
Everywhere we look for smooth round stones,
collect them, add them to the metal trays on our heads.
As they hit the metal they ring out
and dent the scratched steel.

We admire the stream and the fishes
but we are eager to get to the mango tree –
although we are not allowed to go.

When we get there we put our trays down. Laughing.
We don't care that the chickens run to peck our maize,
the goats come to eat our vegetables.
We leave them there, gather our stones and look for the
                mangoes.
The beautiful cherry mangoes like light green
                yellowish plums,
high up, ripe with little seeds inside.

And we gather round the tree in a ring, count
1 – 2 – 3 – and then throw to see who will get
the first lovely, juicy, pretty mango down.
We wait till we are alone because we have been
                warned.
The people come out shouting, blaming us –
'You people from the second village…'
Our stones hit their houses, break their cooking pots.

We go away but can't stop ourselves coming back.
We have to aim high.
We are deaf to everything, we cannot stop.
We look up, watch where the stones go,

see who hits which fruit, dodge the stones coming
        down.
Sometimes I throw wrong deliberately to distract.
Everything is invisible, everything is unreal except the
        mango tree.

I know some will be beaten by the villages –
but that can wait.
I know I will be shouted at –
but that can wait.
I don't think about pain
even though I was beaten yesterday.

The mangoes keep ripening and more come every day.
The more the season comes on, the more beautiful the
        mangoes.
We collect 4 or 5 each and eat them all.
The skin delicate with little dimples all over
like sugar crust and the fruit as warm as blood
I bite deep into the juice.

***

Whatever I do when I am at home I am always in
        trouble.
There is no place for me. But when I am eating
        mangoes,
when I am walking that hot way through the stream,
it's like I'm flying.
This is the place I can show myself, not be shy nor
        quiet,
this is my space, where I can let myself loose.

And I'm not alone there.
Even though the neighbours chase us with canes we
                                    are free,
Brave, ourselves in our own space,
not obedient, not how those who work us,
who beat us and train us, not how they think we are.

Grace Omoloso (Nigeria)

The Waiting Game

Today I went to sign
Today I took the child to school
Today is quiet,
Today is peaceful
Today. No to work
Today I have temporary leave
Today is just what remains.

I take the child to school
I pick the child from school
I go to the shop
I have no money.
I have ... No to work.

I took child to school
I picked the child from school
I went to the shop
I had no money
Again.
I have no permission to work.

At the moment all is quiet.
At the moment it's very peaceful
At the moment I can scream
At the moment I got azure card
At the moment I got temporary leave
Just for the moment,
Just to remain.

Hannah Sabatia (Kenya)

There Was Nothing but Dreams

Dreams of colours, peace and melody.
She could hear people's laughter in the air.
She could feel herself smiling in the dream.

The night was beautiful,
full of scent of flowers
The moon and stars in the sky

The night has passed,
Leaving scorching sun upon her head
Her eyes are blind in the fierce light

Sounds of laughter, smell of success,
Feeling that she belongs:
those sweet dreams all are gone,

The day rose upon her,
she felt nothing but the heat,
Burnt her down to the soul.

The night is back.
It is long and dark night
with no stars on the sky

She is scared to dream again.
Her hands are all blood
from gathering the pieces of dreams

Maria Shafayat (Pakistan)

Trains Passing

It was early morning, and it was just turn to bright but
           still a bit dark.
And it was a cloudy day, very chilly.
I was alone and standing on the platform.
The trains passed very fast.
Some stopped but some not.
They just went pass in front of you
Too fast that you can't see.

I didn't know who was sitting behind the window.
I didn't know what they were doing.
I didn't know what did they think about at that time.

Kaiyun He (China)

What Could Have Been Done More?

What could have been done more?
All the very being of me was standing there tip-toed.

    I was all eye, if you showed something to me
    I was all ear, if you said something to me
    I was all hand, if you asked me do something
    I was all feet, if you wanted me to bring something

    every nerve in my body was active
    not to take signals from me but from you.

    not a day or two,
    not a week or two
    not a month or two,
    not a year or two

    many days and many nights
    in scorching sun
    in heavy rain
    though hail, storm and thunder
    I was standing
    for you, only for you

    not a single part of me was mine
    but I was happy
    that my existence was useful to you
    that I was fulfilling my role.

    I would have remained in my paradise
    until one day I was told
    I never did as much as I should have done.

But how much more?
what more could have been done?

My friend, you are wise
Do you know where I went wrong?

Maria Shafayat (Pakistan)

When I Left

It was summer when I left.
I walked on Tollgate Street
It was Beckton Park
It was calm
It was peaceful.

I saw lots of trees and very beautiful flowers
They had different colours: pink, purple and red
I was looking at my daughter
She was very happy to see the flowers and
She said the smell is very nice.
She looks also like a flower in those flowers.

I like heart touching and calm music
I miss the taste of tea.

***

One day I disappeared from my children for three
            hours.
I went to the beach and walked a long way
Thinking about myself and who I am,
what is the purpose to stay in this world
Looking at the sun it seems very bright, like some
            source of life

I am walking beside the sea and looking at other
            people,
Some are walking, some playing with children
Then suddenly I realise that time that my children

Must be missing me a lot and I should go back to them

I realise my one purpose of my life is to look after my
          children
And give them good morals so that they be good
          humans
In their lives.
My duty is to make my children able to achieve their
          objectives.

Naseem Aslam (Pakistan)

Why Every Human Have Their Own Island?

I'm lost in my life
I am looking for a perfect human to be with me
And I also know that in this world there is no one
                    perfect except God.
Why, why do humans think that life is competition?
Why if others have something you want that?
Why you do what others do?
Why every human have their own island?

I'm lost in my life
I see many people walk in the same road
But some people change their way
And I never see them come back

Naeema al Raisi (Oman)

5.30 a.m., 10 September 2010, Princess of Wales Hospital Bridgend

I heard a baby loudly crying
And at last he was born. My son.
I had waited for him so long.
I put his head on my breast,
his skin on my skin.

I knew 2 women who gave birth before me,
their babies were very beautiful
and I thought mine would be so too.
But he wasn't beautiful –
he was red and crumpled and squashed.
He didn't look like me or my husband.
But I loved him in 2 seconds
because he was my son.

Before I had my husband. Nothing else.
Nowhere to live, no money and no family.
There was no room anywhere for both of us.
We had been staying with people bit by bit
but we could not live together.
Everything was hard and I was so tired.

I was frightened, worried.
There was not enough water for my baby.
He had to be born but the hospitals were full:
there was no space for me to give birth.

When I moved to another hospital
I lay on the bed and everywhere round me was busy

I saw one by one women come into the hospital
and go straight to the labour ward.
But me, I just waited and waited,
one day after one day after one day.

Then one night I was sleeping and
in the dark at midnight, the midwife woke me.
It is your turn now, she said,
I was so happy after waiting so long.

That night my husband was sleeping in the hospital
he had come and gone every day by train and by bus
but that night I was not alone.

The doctor broke my waters
and I was full of pain.
My husband, me and the midwife:
I held their hands so hard I thought I would break
             them.

The midwife was so good to me.
I was frightened. I didn't know what I was doing.
This was my first baby
I was afraid that I would do things wrong.

She encouraged me, she told me all was good.
She told me again and again.
She massaged my head,
She told me I was right
And although the pain was almost insupportable,
that fear of doing wrong was gone.

My husband was holding me

But, after hours of labour, I was drained, exhausted.
I did not eat, just water, and
I didn't have power to push.
Then the midwife put my feet on her shoulders -
and my baby was born.

After I heard my baby cry, I slept.
I was tired, tired after the birth,
tired of my problems.

The midwife spoke gently to me
I could hear her voice and give her a response
but my eyes were so heavy I couldn't open them.
I slept for a long time.

After I gave birth everything difficult was still there.
Every problem still existed.
But it was as if my life was a book
that had turned to a new chapter.

Before we had no family;
then I became a mother
and in two days' time
my son was beautiful
and like my husband as a pea in a pod.

Han Wen Qing (China)

The Door Poems

(i)   *and there he was*

A door opens
And there he was,
Standing about ten yards away.
He called her to come out.
She did not dare.

The child saw him,
Afraid too went away.
They locked the door.

Never saw him again.

(ii) *and he comes in with a mobile in his hand*

A door opens
And he comes in with a mobile in his hand.
Unsure.
The wife is inside with the child.

There is a quarrel.
He has no self-control.
He slaps her on the face.
Slaps her till she passes out.
Slaps her till she passes out
Like dark night the room turns.

She sees stars like in the heavens.

But when she rises up
He is crying as usual,
swearing never again .

Never again.
Never again.

But only for this moment.

(iii)   *and she comes in running*

A door opens
And she comes in running.
A beautiful young girl panting for breath,
Afraid of what has happened.
It was a tense moment.

Hurry up and hide, that's all I could say.
Her masters were fighting.
On this fateful evening
the sun had already gone down.

She had gone to open the gate.
He was drunk, forced her in the car.
He forced her but the wife saw them
She was the house-help,
Loyal and friendly.
She did all her chores.

(iv)   *and we enter one by one*

A door opens,
And we enter one by one.
We are searched head to toe
as one by one we enter.

We must remember all their details,
all the details we want to forget.
Young.
Old.
We sit on the cold long benches,
wait and wait.

Come in here.
Go in there.
Sit by here.
Stand by here.
Do you understand?

All we need is safety
but.
Why did you lie?
Threats
threats.

All we speak is taped,
taped and recorded,
one by one.

(v) *and in comes the chef*

A door opens
And in comes the chef.
Another day of boiled eggs for breakfast.
A year feels like a decade.
The routine and monotony of the hostel
Waiting
And
Waiting
Nobody knowing when decisions will come.

A long day and nothing new.
Out in the endless fields,
Long barbed spiked wire at the edge.

The morning sun a warm blanket.

We take photographs of our long shadows,
They are metres long.
A long day, a long, long day.

Memories of nothing.

(vi)   *and suddenly, with great force,*

A door opens
And suddenly, with great force
They come in twos and fours
With padded chests, chains, sledgehammers, handcuffs
Nikama jitu, hawajali, haja uondoke... *
black uniforms, huge, faceless.

She coils under the bed.
Again under the sofa,
In the cupboard, then tries the shelves.

But the baby cries uncontrollably
Nowhere to hide after all.

* 'Like a giant, they don't care, as long as you get out' (Swahili)

(vii)   and the boy comes in

A door opens
and the boy comes in,
Panting, sweat runs down his face.
He clings to his mother's dress
like he has met her for the first time.

It's raining and cold.
The mother calms him down,
gives him a glass of warm milk.
Slowly the boy speaks
all that his six years has seen.

Excuse me can I play with you?
Excuse me can I play with you?
Excuse me …
can I …
   play
      with
         you?

No boy stops.

School after school.
The other bigger boys run after him.
He is alone, doesn't recall their names.
They all look alike, cool, flicking their fine hair off their
                              faces.

The boy fails to understand.
Mum, what colour am I?

And there are other things he cannot say

Hannah Sabatia (Kenya)

#0061 - 031017 - C0 - 210/148/9 - PB - DID1977460